KATHERINE TINGLEY
Photograph Taken in 1927

THE WISDOM OF THE HEART

Katherine Tingley Speaks

Compiled and Edited by

W. EMMETT SMALL

POINT LOMA PUBLICATIONS, INC.
P.O. Box 9966
San Diego, California 92109

Library of Congress Catalog Card No. 78-65338
ISBN: 0-913004-33

Printed in the United States of America
STOCKTON TRADE PRESS, INC
Norwalk, California 90650

CONTENTS

COMPILER'S PREFACE

The main accomplishments of Katherine Tingley's life are well reported in Emmett A. Greenwalt's *California Utopia, Point Loma*: *1897-1942* not only as leader of the Theosophical Society (Point Loma), but as a forevisioner and practical exponent of things to come: in sound principles of education, in commanding work for world peace, in a plea for prison reform and for abolishment of capital punishment, in her fearless stand for moral and ethical principles. In all these areas, regarded then as largely innovative, voices today alert to deeper values are speaking out.

But perhaps greater comprehension is yet needed of that inner force which was the motivating power behind all Katherine Tingley's acts. That inner force, she declared, was the ancient wisdom, the Theosophy of the ages, inherent in the very fabric of cosmic being. On this she spoke with eloquence, with courage, and with a constancy that was unwavering. Her ringing voice pleaded for a universal brotherhood of humanity, a universal love and understanding based not merely on feeling but on a deep and abiding philosophy which affirms that all peoples, all individuals, are united in that Divine Mystery which is the root and essence of ALL. This was the basic principle of the Theosophical Society which she headed so outstandingly for some thirty-five years and which drew to the theosophical ranks ardent and devoted followers. In her they recognized one who nobly led, who exemplified in the sweep and execution of program those qualities of leadership that caught the imagination of varied but stalwart and independent minds as well as devoted and loving hearts. It was the wisdom of universality that drew from them this response, a driving irresistible force that spoke to both heart and mind and told them here was something worth living for, something the world needs, sound and true and lasting because based on the Theosophia of the ages, both cosmic and human. Here was Truth, as near as human mind and heart can reach to, spoken in words understandable to child and adult and translated into practical action.

But Katherine Tingley's work lay beyond the confines of a theosophical organization. It reached out to touch that universal theosophical Movement to which many are allied though perhaps unknown to themselves. Her words inspired recognition of an inner beauty, what she would call the light of the soul. She spoke to the heart of the people, overleaping biases of religious beliefs, predilections or ingrained parochial tradition, to reach what is quintessential to the very heart of Being itself.

Katherine Tingley who lived the first fifty years of her life in the last century was able to understand its problems; and living in the next three decades of the 20th century she was able to do something about those problems, to expose their causes and offer a cure. What she accomplished, as we look back on those crowded years, amounts to a challenge, an adjuration, a veritable invocation to all that is highest and spiritual in man to so fill his everyday duties that the inner light to which she appealed will shine and illumine his every action.

In Theosophy, she declared, we find the solution of all the problems that vex the sober thinking mind. It points the way to the right treatment of the downtrodden and outcast of humanity, and it offers the real remedies for poverty, vice and crime. It shows the fallacy of war, for which the only cure are regeneration and the application of universal ideals. It declares that unbrotherliness is the insanity of the age; that ethics are rooted in the universe; that we are responsible for all our thoughts and actions and reap only what we sow; that death has a beauty we can learn to understand, and that life after life brings that needed renewal and opportunity for growth which can see the realization of our highest hopes.

Her philosophy urges a practice in action. There is no need, she pleads, to live in the lesser self. Dare to be your greater self. It does not take a lifetime, it does not take a year, for a man to discover the god within himself. If he has the courage to face the issues he may find it in a moment of time. That moment can bring revelation, a linking of oneself to a divine and greater consciousness. There is an immediacy in this that brooks no hesitation or faltering, but seizes upon and makes part of one's own being that indefinable something to which we aspire. Words cannot express it. Only the silence fully speaks. Only the wisdom of the heart can hear and feel and realize. —These were the commandments, we might say, Katherine Tingley uttered.

Fifty years have passed. The world is more ready now to understand. Those who knew Katherine Tingley well will read these pages, we feel, with sound renewal. Those who have not known her or perhaps have misunderstood her have here the opportunity for new perceptions and wiser assessment. Here she speaks—not only for her time, but for today, and for the centuries to come. Listen!

W. Emmett Small

1978

PUBLISHER'S NOTE

July 11, 1979, will mark the fiftieth anniversary of Katherine Tingley's "passing into Light". In anticipation of this date, Point Loma Publications, Inc., is happy to publish this book: a compilation of extracts from her lectures given during many years of her public life, as well as instructions to her students and other relevant material. This should provide to a larger circle of earnest readers the essence of her inspired teaching.

1

NATURE THE MIGHTY MOTHER

Beyond the Veil of Visible Things

A Knowledge Evoked From Within

The Silence and Its Song

NATURE THE MIGHTY MOTHER

Beyond the Veil of Visible Things

I looked out over the blue waters of the Pacific; I watched the sun rise above the mountains and listened to a mocking-bird singing; and the beauty of the awakening world grew marvelous for me with suggestions of the hidden harmonies of life. Then I thought of humanity, and wondered what would happen could the veil of external things fall from before our eyes and reveal the glory of the Law. We should stand in silence motionless, thrilled through with the grace and plentitude of its compassion.

Long ago there was a time when men lived in purity of thought and act, and knew little of selfishness, and moved through the experiences of their incarnations not bound down or interfered with as the human mind is today. Better than we do they understood how to conduct their lives. There was not the rush and whirl of things. They lived more inwardly, in communion with what is best and noblest. The splendor of spiritual life was manifest, and through all human consciousness shone deepest reverence for Nature and truth. Better than we do, too, they knew how to work with Nature; and found in her something the people of modern times have never discovered.

But today how many are satisfied with their lives, or sure that they possess the truth, or know whence they came when they were born, or, after death, whither they are going? Yet there is a promise in our hearts and in the Divine Law that all that mankind has been shall be again; and all that we have forgone we shall recover.

We lost touch ages ago with the Mighty Mother, Nature, and now need to go to her again, for the most part, in her forests or on her hilltops or by the seashore, to find our own souls in her quiet places, and to learn that all matter responds to the spiritual touch. Out beyond hearing and seeing and thinking are infinite Laws that control our lives, divine Laws that hold us in their keeping; and immediately behind the veil of visible things, and but a little way from the consciousness of our mortal selves, are Higher Forces at work for our good.

They speak to the soul to make the way broad and beautiful. They speak to us at all times through the sunlit sky and the starlight; the shining silences of Nature proclaim to us always the greatness of the world and the hidden grandeur of man, so that in the desert, in the deep caverns of the earth, under the heaviest weight or sorrows "he that hath ears to hear" is never alone. And were he lost in the great waste places, or in a rudderless boat on the open sea, or were he on the brink of created things and far from the world of men, he would carry within him still the Kingdom of Heaven and might find in his heart all the revelations for which humanity is longing.

It is the Spiritual Message that the world is crying for, a baptism of the spirit of the Divinity of Man, whereby we should be made to realize that the heavens are opening to our needs, that the light is breaking and new stars are shining, that the things we do not see are greater than the things we see—what the heart yearns for, more than we know; that Nature is supremely just, and in all this grand universal Scheme of Being not a thought, not an aspiration, not the smallest effort is lost or wasted.

We cannot succeed unless we work with Nature, who will not accept half-hearted service. We receive no answer when we call to her only in moments of dilemma or disappointment, and then turn again and desert her. She has no word for the insincere or indifferent; she responds only to those whose minds are awake to the highest aims.

You who are despairing, who have little faith in yourselves or hope of tomorrow, or belief that you can control your conditions, seek aid here of the Great Mother. Look up into the blue sky or the stars; catch in the air the feeling of her universal life. And then examine yourselves, and discover that many of your sorrows have come to you because you have not been willing to suffer. I find treasures of experience in suffering. Any real attainment must come through discipline; and no matter how it may be outwardly, we can meet it as that which will call forth the stronger side of us, until it becomes at last the very joy of our lives and we love it as we love the sunshine and the aroma of flowers.

Fear is the basis of all discouragement. Only cultivate fearlessness in meeting the trials from without and the weaknesses within, and you cease to be alone; you attain discernment of a grand companionship ever present with you, and become aware of the God that is within you and yet without you, the Everywhere-existing whose voice you may hear, listening for it, in your own spirit, and no less in the murmur of the brooks and in the birds' chorusings, for the Mystery in the heart of Nature is also the Mystery in the heart of Man, and the same wonderful powers are in both.

The secret of life is impersonal love. It is impersonality that is our great need today; impersonality wins her secrets from the Mystic Mother. If we dismiss the idea of a personal god, and dismiss our own personalities with all their limitations and misgivings; if we carry our minds beyond self into the limitless, our thought into the universal order; and from the inmost recesses of our consciousness regard the universe in its magnificence, until, lifted out of ourselves, we recognize within ourselves greater things than ever we have dreamed of and draw near to inspirations unendingly beautiful and rich; and make question then as to the interpretation of it and the meaning of all these limitless rhythms of life and order that throng the immensity of space—her answer will come back to us. We shall behold the universe as the outgrowth, the expression, of an infinite scheme proceeding from an Inmost Source beyond our comprehension—the Fountain, the Center, the Unknowable Absolute Light: flowing out from Which, following the plan of evolutionary law, passing through the many lives ordained for our growth towards perfection—we are here to work out the purposes of existence.

A Knowledge Evoked From Within

Godlike qualities lie sleeping within us, the spiritual things that mark us immortal. For here within the heart is the Kingdom of Heaven, and the only recompense a man needs is to become aware of his own divinity. It is there, a creative power within us, by whose virtue he who has patience to endure and work shall behold the fruit of his efforts—the human family glorified and brought to the goal his heart tells him may be reached. An order of life shall yet be established by those who have gone through the schools of experience, birth after birth, round after round, until they lifted themselves out of the strain and sorrow. Their building will be of a new kind, a type of civilization higher than anything we have read or imagined. The minds of men will expand in the atmosphere of universal brotherhood; earth will give up its secrets and the stars declare the mighty mystery of their lives; things of old unheard of will come from the hearts of men; we shall hear the answer to the pleadings of the advance-guard.

How many believe it possible to establish the Kingdom of Heaven upon earth? The majority, even of the so-called spiritually-minded, carry their thoughts into far spaces when they think of it. Yet it is here within the heart. It is in man; it is on earth, and we can come into it because we are part of the Universal Scheme. The grandeur of creation, and all that vast quietude above us, the mysterious sublimity we look out upon, proclaim to us *that which no man sees, none regards, and that this earth is the paradise of God, the place of souls or angels, the gate of heaven.* And yet we have seen in the flowers and in the stars only that part of them which many have seen; and heard but what many have heard in the winds and in the roaring of the sea. There are millions of lights in heaven we have never caught sight of; there are millions of planets evolving; and wonders in the world around us of which we have never conceived.

There is no limit to the possible expansion of human life and the growth of the Soul. The Soul is not a thing to be set aside and as it were locked up for awhile and brought out upon occasions. It is that nobler part of our nature that rises to every situation and meets it with patience and courage; it is the power that often sweeps into a man's life unaware and carries him out beyond all brain-mind thought into the great broad road of service. It must be given breadth and scope and the large environment it demands. The knowledge of it comes not in any world-startling or magical way, and is not to be purchased save by the surrender of a man's passionate and lustful nature to the God within. It is a knowledge that steals upon us in the quiet of the night-time and in all our peaceful moments, when we serve our fellows and ask for no reward but the glory that shines through the silence in him who has done his utmost, and the peace of mind that is for those who are striving. Through our smallest actions it may enter, when we are at our best and in love with what is truest and noblest, when we are in despair yet cling to our high ideals and dreams. Something comes home to us then and we say, *This will of mine is free that but now wavered and was surrounded and oppressed;*

I can look with perfect trust into tomorrow and into eternity.

It is a knowledge that must be evoked from within. Each must earn it through his own efforts. It cannot be conveyed in words; the greatest of seers could not explain it, nor the greatest of orators make it clear. Each must find within himself the light and the key, the fire and redemptive stimulation, making his mind free and receptive as the flowers to the sunlight. But let a man seek it for his own sake, and all his efforts will amount to nothing. He must do it for the salvation of the race, aware that there is no separateness on the inner planes; that we are all brothers and our brothers' keepers, and that not until we get real knowledge of the inner self in ourselves can we interpret our other selves, our fellow-men. We must understand the delicate and intricate interaction and functioning of the different parts of our own being before we can claim understanding of the laws of universal life.

The Silence and Its Song

At any moment in every life the hour of revelation may be at hand. It requires no epoch or special season, nor the beginning or end of any outer cycle. In regions within ourselves where intellect is not, but imagination has full scope for its greatness, we touch the Infinite off and on at all times, and stand on the brink of vast possibilities and truths. We can draw upon resources greater than we dream of.

Imagination is not the peculiar property of men of genius and exceptional talent, but a power innate in everyone, and that which might help each to find his Soul. It is the hand-maiden of the God in man, and our guide into that Kingdom of Heaven within, which is the realm of thought where the Soul speaks to the heart and mind—in the silent places of our lives, in the moments when we verge upon greatness, when an overwhelming consciousness comes in upon us of the universality of the Divine Life, and of the divine possibilities latent in man; when the silences of great Nature cry to us tidings of the God in ourselves, and we feel the nearness, the companionship, of That which it would be presumption to define, but in whose universal presence we must tinge our thoughts and feelings with a certain solemnity, a mystery and grandeur . . . before the Mirror of this Infinite Beauty, in the Temple of this Majesty, standing in an attitude of larger reverence . . . in silence.

In silence we must stand—to gather out of that solemn beauty the joy humanity needs. Much more can be expressed through silence than through speech. The inner life which is music—the overtones and undertones of the universal harmony—is only accessible in the silence. Music lifts for awhile the veil between ourselves and the Unseen, the Unspoken, the Unknowable; but there is a music that cannot be heard, that the heart can feel and the soul realize and the mind reach to, so potent that it is without outward sound.

Before ever man was on earth, Nature, dwelling alone in her beauty and secret mysterious power, felt the need of some grander manifestation of Divinity, and as it were cried aloud to the Higher Law to bring a new power into the world; and in answer to her prayer Man stepped into the arena of life—Man the Master, thrilled through and held and controlled by the Divine Spark, the spiritual center of his being. Then when thus the Human Soul was first incarnate here, out of its own inmost depths and out of the heart of the deep silences of Nature a glorious song arose that swept and echoed through the universe,

> "*The stars of Morning sang together,*
> *And all the Sons of God shouted for joy*"—

the Soul of Man and the Soul of Nature singing in harmony; and the song became assimilated with the silence of the stars and the mountains and the murmur of the forests and the seas, and has sung itself down since through all the reaches of time, its magical overtones heard in our hearts, reminding us of our lost godhood, of our goal which is perfection, and of the unflinching courage proper to us as souls.

Only in the silent and secret recesses of our being can we hear it. Only there can truth be fully known. When the outer senses are stilled, and self-control takes possession of the mind, listening inwardly, one may hear the deeper notes of the divine melody. It works on inner and quiet lines; touches our consciousness here and there, quickening it to greater sensitivity. Our outer ears are deaf to it because we have willed them away from hearing. Our minds cannot perceive, because with our indifference we have rebuked the Higher Law, and allowed the confused thoughts of the lower man, mean or doubting, to keep us in the shadows. And yet I know that wherever we might be, in the darkest corner of the earth or the most beautiful, were our senses not dulled with the noise of the world we should hear the Grand Symphony.

Go back in thought to the time of your childhood, when the world was beautiful to you, and such appreciation of the fulness of life came over you that your inmost soul told you of its own divine nature, and you felt in your heart the presence of God. You caught the sound, inwardly, of the mighty overtones and overtones then! To all of us such moments of revelation come.

As a child in the woods of my father's estate in New England I learned to love the silence. There was always a song for me in the noiseless waters of the historic Merrimac as they swept along the woodland shores towards the sea. The quiet of friendly pine trees soothed my unrest. They seemed to me dear companiones of my own, set there to guard the secrets of Nature. The birds in my imaginings were darling wood-fairies, messengers from some inner and lovelier land. The fragrance of the pines and laurels was the breath of the Great Spirit, the Love that brooded over all things. I felt as though I were some winged thing. At unexpected moments a Master-Power awakening within me filled my brain with pictures that came and went. It spoke to me through the silence of the pines; and when a bird chirped or a small breeze stirred the branches, the sound blended in my thought with infinity and became for me a message from the Divinity within.

It all came back when I went up into those same woods at 'The Laurels' again a few years ago. The old beauty was there, and the feeling of the infinite life above and about me and the Infinite Presence I could trust—THAT that is all-beauty, the Reality, the Reality behind this world of appearances, the Supreme beyond the range of thought. I felt through sun and trees and river the immeasurable joy that flows towards us forever through shining Nature and her silence.

And then came a pang because humanity will not believe, since it does not hear and see; and will not listen for the great Song of Life, and is shut out from all this sacredness, and dwells exiled and oblivious in this radiant universe its spiritual home, and knows nothing of the inward beauty, the symphonies that are yet unheard, the divinity that thrills through ourselves and all things.

2

RECOLLECTIONS

On the Banks of the Merrimac

The Civil War

East Side New York

India and the Teacher's Words

Egypt and the Tomb of the Pharaohs

RECOLLECTIONS

On the Banks of the Merrimac

I go back in thought to my childhood days, far back, into the State of Massachusetts, on the banks of the historic Merrimac River, immortalized by the American Quaker poet John Greenleaf Whittier. There I spent my childhood days on my father's estate. I lived far away from the rush and whirl of city life.

On one side of my family they were strong members of the Congregational Church, and on the other side they were materialists. I was the only daughter in the family, and even between five and six years of age I found myself questioning and studying the great mystery of life. I looked upon nature as one of God's greatest gifts. Young as I was I realized its mystery, its wonder, its superb silence, its dignity, its life, and its teaching. I learned to love nature, the flowers, the birds, the blue sky, and all. My young life was spent largely with nature, in the woods, over the hills, in my boat, along the country waysides on horseback, and in other out-of-door sports. At that time it was considered very disgraceful for a young girl to attempt to row a boat or to ride a horse astride or to swim. I was severely criticized sometimes for indulging in these innocent pleasures. A precise religious maiden-lady of the Puritan order promised that my life would be a very unpleasant one, and that everything would go wrong with me because I did some things a little outside the conventionalities of church-life.

I never knew what fear was. I remember the first time I heard the name of God mentioned I was so disappointed and set back and almost discouraged to think that the

God that I had learned to love in nature, the God I had learned to love with all my soul, without any teachings was, according to the preachments of man, "a revengeful and a punishing God." This set me thinking. I kept on thinking and am still thinking and am still wondering and regretting that this is believed by many. Yet I still believe in the Eternal, Supreme, All-Powerful Light—the Source, Center, and All-Compassionate Giver of all that is true and noble in life. This is my God.

As I grew older, went off to boarding-school and came back to my home, and then went out into the world, married, and lived for many years in New York City, there were daily pictures before me that were so despairing, so disappointing, so beyond endurance for a human mind like mine. I saw the poverty on the East Side of New York City. I saw the street-woman. I went to the prisons and saw the unfortunates there. I read in the newspapers of men being hanged. And then I began to recognize when not so very old that men do not tell each other what they think of each other. I began to think that all men wore masks in order to hide their real selves.

Finally I realized that these insincerities were the result of man's limited views of life. If a man believes in only one life, and if he believes in a punishing God he must have fear, he cannot have a proper understanding of his own divine nature, of the majesty of the soul, its power, and his future, his responsibilities. Why? Because he has yet a limited picture of life—one earth-life only.

But all this changes when we can take, as Theosophists do, the broad picture of human life and believe that under all these outer aspects, all these disappointing features, all the heart-ache, the agony, the vice, and the crime of the world, there is within every man the divine part of his nature, and that this divinity is a part of God.

Back of the imaginings and hopes and dreams of my childhood and womanhood, deeper than the pain caused by the contrasts I have observed in human life, there is a consciousness of the love of God and the spiritual dignity of man. And it is this consciousness that is needed now to make the world better, to bring man to his own, to give him the key to life's problems, so that he can combat difficulties understandingly, overcome injustice through knowledge, and live in the joy of life in the truest and noblest sense.

The Civil War

It was when the Civil War broke out that I first came in contact with the horror of war. It was in 1861. In Massachusetts my father had recently organized a company and brought it to Virginia, where his regiment, the New York Mozart, was stationed on the road to Fairfax. And soon afterwards my mother and the rest of us followed, and lived for awhile in an old mansion in Fairfax County so as to be near him.

Along the road we traveled on the way there, thousands of forest-trees had been felled by the axmen; trenches had been thrown up in every direction, and in the distance forts could be seen everywhere. Everywhere, too, there were thousands of soldiers, some drilling, some lounging around in their tents, but all with the stern, set and strained expression on their faces that made me think, even then, of the many tragedies of the battles they had fought and still were to fight.

I used to go riding with my eldest brother into camp and along the line where many of the regiments were stationed; and it was always these grim, horror-stricken faces that impressed me. Everything in the war-atmosphere had something of misery in it that awed me, and there seemed to be no remedy.

After the second battle of Bull Run, I saw the ambulance returning with the dead and dying, followed by files of Confederate soldiers, ragged and half starving, sick and war-worn, pushed along by the Union men who had them in charge to the old Capitol Prison.

I remember another time one night just after the Seven Days Battle before Richmond when the soldiers were trying to reach the encampment outside Alexandria. At that time we were staying in that city, and Ellsworth's Zouaves were bivouacked in the street in front of our home. I can see them still in the glare of the pine-torches. I had gotten out of bed and stood at the window in the dark room looking out on it all. And there the wounded came straggling in. They had been marching all day from the front, caring for their wounds as best they might. The Medical Staff, as I remember it, was being brought up from the rear to meet them there in Alexandria, and had not yet arrived. And suddenly I could stand it no longer. I summoned my old colored mammy and made her come down into the kitchen with me, and there we took charge of things somehow and requisitioned anything and everything that I could, and went out to the soldiers. Hours later I was missed, and my father found me at midnight in the street among the soldiers binding up their wounds.

I think it was just after Bull Run, when McClellan took command of the scattered forces of the Union and began to reorganize them on the Potomac, that I came into a full realization of the vileness and terror of war. I had heard the deadly cannonading in the distance and known that human beings were being mowed down by thousands. It had been for me a phantom of horror.

It was the day of the grand review of the Army of the Potomac; and my brother and I witnessed that imposing spectacle. McClellan was there; and so was President Lincoln and thousands of onlookers from Washington and elsewhere. I remember seeing Secretary Seward among the other officials. Eighty thousand infantry, eight thousand calvary and about twenty batteries of artillery made up the pageant, in those days one that was considered remarkable indeed. But all their splendid array brought nothing but tears to my heart and eyes, for crowding on my mind incessantly came pictures of what had been, what was to be, why they were there. I looked out on it all in despair. My heart went out in equal tenderness to the South and the North with as deep sympathy for the one side as for the other. They were all martyrs to the insanity of the age, the insanity of unbrotherliness which had brought about that, as it brings about every, war. Picture after picture came before my mind's eye of the end and aim of it all, and question upon question filled my thoughts. How could the divine spirit of brotherly love prevail to sustain the Negro Race in its real advancement if it had not prevailed to avert the slaughter? I had little heart to think of the alleged glory of war, the trappings and the pageantry, the "splendor of the captains and the shouting". What filled my vision was man's inhumanity to man, and the dire need of a new gospel or revelation from the great Center of Light to call a halt to warfare then and bring about that by which it might be abolished forever.

Many years have passed since then, but humanity has not yet learned wisdom.

East Side New York

Some years before coming in touch with the Theosophical Movement I was living in New York. I had a comfortable home and no children. My love of children was very great and my love of the unfortunate also. So I began to work in the prisons; I worked with women on the street, and for the drunkards and the poverty-stricken, the starving and the sick. I was happy to do it. I neglected none of my duties. I did every duty as conscientiously as I could. But I could not enjoy life. I dared not face my conscience without doing something more to lift the weight of the burdens from the suffering people.

So my work carried me down to the East Side of New York City where thousands of people come in from different countries — the immigrants, thinking when they come that America is the open door to wealth and prosperity. They find themselves in very small quarters, in very limited surroundings, very many of them go hungry and suffer much, and thus they lose faith in humanity. It was among these that I worked.

Long before I became Leader of the Theosophical Movement (Point Loma) I had seen much to convince me that we do not know what remedies to use for the crime of poverty of the age, nor how to apply them. A terror grew in my heart, and I became sick and discouraged, because I saw so much cruelty and indifference, so much suffering and so little done to relieve it. To establish schools of prevention—that was my dream. And it was not born in a day, but came after long experience of work among the destitute in New York, mostly on the East Side. It was impressed on my mind during many visits to the prisons there, and to Ellis Island; and in much rescue work among the unfortunates of the streets.

It was plain to see that little could be done really and permanently to help them. What was needed was a new system of education for the prevention of the conditions I met. To recognize human nature when it had already lost faith and become awry and twisted, skeptical and cynical, seemed almost or quite impossible. I saw that the only way was to mold the characters of the children, in the plastic first seven years of their lives, and then on, somewhat differently, from seven to fourteen.

These thoughts and feelings grew acute one bitter winter when the East Side was seriously affected by a strike of the cloakmakers. Day after day these people were holding out for what they considered their rights, and the destitution had become terrible. They had no resources left, and their children were on the point of starvation. One morning a baby died in its mother's arms at the door of the Do-Good Mission, an emergency relief society I had established, with its headquarters in an old tenement house in the region of great privation. Crowds used to come there daily for soup and bread and what else I could provide to help them.

I remember that day well. Snow was falling when I started out in the morning to go down to the Mission to meet those discouraged persons in their poverty—an ordinary snow-storm that gave little warning of the tremendous blizzard that was to rage later in the day, and the fury of which was beginning to be apparent when I arrived. And in that fierce storm, now increasing momentarily, over six hundred women and children were waiting in the street for relief. They were but half-dressed; they had pawned most of their clothes; they were perishing with the cold; they were wailing out loud, many of them, and clamoring for help.

The rooms we had taken were on the first floor, the best we could get, though the house was old and ramshackle; and to have brought or tried to bring those six hundred in would have meant death for most or all of them. The landlord had warned me most peremptorily that the floor would hardly bear the weight of fifty without collapsing and falling into the cellarage. And all the while the cry of those women was ringing in my ears. I could not send them away hungry; and it would be some little time yet before the food that was being prepared would be ready.

There was nothing for it but for me to go out and talk to them, to keep them as well as I could in humor and patience while waiting. So I had a large grocery box placed on the sidewalk beside the door; and standing on it, told them why I could not ask them in, and that the soup was not yet quite cooked, and the bread not yet delivered from the baker's; but in a very short time both would be ready.

And all the while the crowd and the storm kept increasing; and with them, my own distress, till I felt my heart almost at breaking-point to see so much keen misery and to know that all I could do was so wretchedly little, so ineffectual to lift them out of their present trouble and keep them secure against as bad or worse tomorrow or the next day.

And then it was that suddenly my attention was caught by a pale face on the outskirts of the crowd, the face of a man standing under an umbrella, with his coat-collar turned up and buttoned round his neck, and his hat low down over his face—clearly not one of the strikers, a gentleman, I thought, suddenly reduced to destitution and ashamed to come forward with the rest and ask for the food he sorely needed; a face fine of features and strikingly noble of expression, with a look of grave sadness, too, and of sickness, caused by hunger no doubt, I thought. All this flashed through my mind in that one glance; and I turned to call one of our attendants to send her to him; but when I looked round again he was gone.

Two days later he presented his card at my home. It was William Quan Judge, leader of the Theosophical Movement in America and H. P. Blavatsky's successor. He told me he had read of my work among the poor, and had gone down there to see it for himself. He had found it, so far, practical and valuable, he said; but also had divined my discontent with it, and my hunger for something that would go much deeper, removing the causes of misery and not merely relieving the effect.

It was then, when I came to know him, that I realized I had found my place. I was face to face with a new type of human nature, with something akin to that which my inner consciousness had told me a perfect human being might be. The more I became acquainted with him and with his work, the more I felt assured that some of my old dreams and hopes might yet come true. Fully and accurately to describe him would be beyond my power, he so stood out above the run of men in deep wisdom and lofty nobility of character. He had made Theosophy the living power in his life, and none could be so bitter against him as to exhaust his tolerance or his compassion.

A prophet is without honor in his own country; and William Q. Judge suffered persecution, and his life was shortened by it. But I wonder whether, if he had come from the Far East in the white robe of a swami, two-thirds of the American people would not have been on their knees to him. It was he who first gave me glimpses of the power of thought, and made me realize what it will do to build or ruin the destiny of a human being. And in so doing he showed me how to find in Theosophy the solution of all the problems that had vexed me; how it points the way to the right treatment of the down-trodden and outcast of humanity, and to the real remedies for poverty, vice, and crime.

On all these subjects the first word of Theosophy is this: He who would enter upon the path that leads to truth must put new interpretations on the failings and mistakes of his fellow-men. He must come to understand the Law of Eternal Justice—Karma, that "whatsoever a man soweth, that shall he also reap"; and to know the necessity it implies for an unconquerable compassion. Because those who fail and fall short do so always through ignorance. Crime is always the result of ignorance, and there can be no cure for it until this is recognized.

India and the Teacher's Words

I remember vividly the morning I met H. P. Blavatsky's Teacher on the mountainside near Darjîling. He was dressed plainly in the Tibetan style and had an English pocket-knife in his hand and was whittling a piece of wood with it. In the field below, not far away, a young Hindu was plowing with a brace of oxen, and the whittling I was told was to make a little plug or peg which, inserted in the yoke, would make it easier for the beasts.

He drew my attention to the plowman, one of his own chelas, and this is the substance of what he said.

Were a battery of guns firing and the shells falling all around him he would not stir from his work. Indeed, he would hardly be aware of the noise or the peril so absorbed he is. Those two oxen with anyone else are most unmanageable creatures; with him they are always, as now, perfectly quiet. He does not control them with his will. His mind does not concern itself with them at all; but you see there for yourself proof that those dumb things can feel the atmosphere of purity of thought. And when he goes upon a pilgrimage he will travel more miles in a day than any of the others and come in far ahead. You know how the women here in India lave and anoint the feet of the pilgrims? Well, his feet after the longest day's journey have never been found hurt or damaged by the road. Why? Because he never dreads or even thinks of the distance, but goes on his way happily; and it never occurs to him to be troubled as to whether or not he may have missed the road or taken the wrong turning. His mind is so buyoant with the joy of the spiritual life that it actually lightens his body for him.

You know, the atoms of the human body become weighed down as a rule with the burdens of the mind, the irrelevant ideas, the preoccupations and anxieties. They go through series of changes momentarily, affected by the thoughts of the brain-mind. The lack of trust, the lack of inspiration that people suffer from, the hopelessness, brings these atoms down half way to death. But they can be quickened to a kind of immortality by the fire of the divine life, and attuned into universal harmony. Men anywhere could get rid of all that burden of unnecessities, and carry themselves like that young chela does if they had the mental balance.

If you had to go from here to America you would not sit still and dream about the place you wanted to go to, and think that was enough. The trouble with some theosophical aspirants is that they waste the strength of their lives looking at the goal ahead rather than at the immediate moments and seconds of which the Path is composed; and so their better selves become exhausted. They should let the Beaming Thought pour itself into each arriving moment and be indifferent to the morrow. One can find in every instant of time, if one has the desire, the door into worlds of golden opportunity, the gateway to a glorious path stretching out into the limitless Eternal.

To move away from the material plane of effort and thought and personality, that is what the soul is urging us to do: to move out into the hidden vast realities of life and understand that within and above and around us, and in the very atmosphere in which our thoughts and feelings exist, Universal Life is pulsating continuously in response to our yearnings and questionings. When people say that they are seeking happiness they mean that they are aiming at that stage in their evolution where their present problems will be solved. To reach it one must withdraw from the allurements of life and all its outward and discouraging aspects, and find himself in the solitude of his own being, in a silence unbreakable within his own heart and mind.

The outer life is transient. He must gain the inner power and live in the Spirit which is eternal. He cannot step free-souled into that light without having learned concentration, which many these days advertise they can teach, and lecture on it, forming cults, holding classes, and taking dollars. But all they can do at last is to lead their victims away from reality and farther and farther away from the True Self within themselves. For concentration is a power inherent in the Self and above and beyond the mind. It cannot be found in the objective world, for it is not there. The Kingdom of Heaven is on earth, and the gates of it are to be sought and discovered in the heart of man.

So the aspirant should not think about the cultivation of powers, but live in the light and strength of his own Higher Nature. The Divine Law is in every man and woman, and each must find it there for himself and make it manifest in his life. No one can pour pure water into foul so that it shall still retain its purity. Selflessness attains; selfishness defeats; men's possibilities are in direct proportion to their ability to see beyond themselves and to feel for others.

To throw the mind, on moving out of sleep into waking, directly upon the outward things, is to lose half the life of the day. One should awake in the morning with a beautiful thought, reminding himself that the battle for the day is before him, and that the God Within desires a moment's conference with the mind before the arduous duties of the morning begin. He should find something in the silence and sunlight of the first hours which should link itself with his own Higher Nature and bring forth the blossom and the fruit. He should free himself in the morning in the sweetness of the sunlight, beginning the day as gently as though he were waking a little child from its slumbers, bringing forward the truer and nobler side of himself—not working it out in words and language, but in thought approaching the richness and fulness of the Spirit and letting the God Within blossom each moment as it rises. Then, reaching out for the most difficult duty that one *knows to be one's duty*, and overcoming it, he will learn the secret of being on guard, and in a little while have thrown away unawares the burdens that obstructed him. Many have been working hard and conscientiously to get rid of these burdens. There is no need to spend a moment on them. It is but to put aside the doubts and misgivings, to enter the chambers of the Soul, to bask in the sunlight and strength that are there.

The first three hours of the day are the great opportunity. He who does not rise with the sun loses an immense amount of power. He who rises before the sun and by daybreak has finished with the duties of this plane and what may be necessary for the care of the body, and is ready to step out with the sunrise and work with the sun—he has the co-operation of a force he little knows of—the vibrant blue light behind the sun.

The trouble is with many aspirants that too often they begin with the letter and go backwards in search of the spirit. But let them hold to these things in the silence going alone in the morning into the silence of Nature, freeing themselves from their old trying memories and from all anticipations of trouble. And it will not hurt them to look at the stars with wonder occasionally; or to listen with delight to the music of the birds; or to spend whole days in silence, brooding on these sacred things whilst performing all the duties that come to them to do. . . .

This was in substance what the Teacher had to say. I think he placed a talisman in our hands and gave us the real secret of life.

Egypt and the Tomb of the Pharaohs

I remember how the wonder and power of Theosophy were born in upon me on my first visit to Egypt. There the footsteps of the ancient times are visible, and the truth men lived and brooded of old endures still and cannot die. In the clear motionless air, in the mountains and old temples, there is a silence and an impress of ages gone which awaken the imagination. One feels the presence and potency of the truths that shone through the Mysteries of old, and that the great hierophants and Teachers have left the touch of their inner lives in the atmosphere. Those silent hills, worn with age, how they spoke to me! They were full of the mightiness of ancient times and the spiritual activities of the great Egyptians. The old Nile talked to me, and the moon above the Nile, until I knew that the greatest and most eloquent power in Nature as well as in human life is silence.

It was borne in upon me in the tombs of the Pharaohs. I remember the day when we rode from Luxor along the bank of the river and up over hills and down through ravines, and then walked through a door in the hillside, and by galleries and galleries underground, and by flights of stairs carved in the rock, and into a room lit with electricity—the tomb of Seti I.

The mummy was there. The lid of the sarcophagus had been removed and the lights were disposed so that one could see the great king's features. As we went in there and looked at the face of that mighty monarch, one of the very greatest of the Pharoahs, a silence seemed to descend upon the whole party, an inner and majestic silence, which was in itself a symphony of symphonies, as if we had been ushered into the presence of something that still remained, and was in its essence imperishable, of that long-dead ruler's greatness.

There were many periods anciently when the Soul was better understood than it is now and when men fashioned their lives simply and beautifully in accordance with the magnificent aspirations of Nature, when they listened for and heard, as we do but very rarely, the melody of life which is the voice of the Inner Divinity; when they talked with the stars, and had no fear written on their faces; when they knew no dogmas at all, nor fear of death, nor spiritual nor mortal terror.

All that was best in the history of those early races is here now in the very atmosphere in which we live. It is not lost. It is in Nature. It has made itself a part of the harmony of universal life.

3

PEACE AND THE FALLACY OF WAR

PEACE AND THE FALLACY OF WAR

War and preparation for war and thought towards war —these are a confession of weakness. To maintain peace is a proof and manifestation of strength. I would not dare criticize the patriotism of any honest man, or reflect in any way on those who do what they think is their duty, but a man's foes are they of his own household, and so it is with a nation. Our enemies are not outside but within, in our own national mind and customs, our national aggressions and fallings short. We distrust our neighbors because we distrust ourselves. I do not mean in this or that nation alone, but all over the world. We might all of us talk less about being proud of our countries, and work more for their spiritual advancement and regeneration.

It is universal ideals that the world is aching for today. We need to understand as never before that our responsiblities are not for ourselves alone, not for our own countries alone, but for the whole human family. Territory and trade may be much; national honor may be much; but the general salvation of human society here in this world, that is ALL.

The most vital need of every people on earth is permanent peace, and to get permanent peace we must create and sustain an international spirit or world-patriotism which will come as the result of recognition that what affects one nation affects all, that as far as one ascends towards knowledge and well-being, so far all others will follow; that as deep as one may fall away from its ideals and into national selfishness, to that depth, or lower, in the nature of things the others will be dragged down too; that each nation must partake of the good and bad karma of all.

In a country that based its life wholly on principle and the spirit of human brotherhood, patriotism would be altogether a noble thing, and its aim would not be to set hearts beating at the sound of a drum, but to induct all minds into conceptions of the meaning of life. Were each nation to cultivate patriotism and national loyalty of that type the world would soon be united in a universal beneficent system.

National interests ought to be dear to us, so dear that we should be eager to give our lives—in the living, not in the dying—to preserve the reality, the inner life and spiritual beauty of our countries, to protect the future generations and leave them a heritage of noble life, an incorruptible dignity of culture such as money cannot purchase nor brute force attain or defend.

The highest law of our being demands that we should build our nations on the rock of that enduring wisdom which belongs to the Divine Soul of Man, and rear our children accordingly, that they and their posterity after them may not know the sorrows we have known, but build on the rich results of our strivings the foundation of the great Republic of the Soul, that Inner Republic of which all souls are citizens, that it may be established "on earth as it is in heaven." But to stand merely and narrowly for one's own country is a suicidal substitute for patriotism. It is, eventually, a poisoning of the supposed object of its devotion because it implies working against the general life and spiritual health of the world, on which the life and spiritual health of each nation depend. We cannot separate ourselves from humanity.

The curse of our nations is separateness. We are not agreed upon any scheme of life or thought or action. We are separated one from another by the imaginary interests of daily life, and competition carried too far is ringing the death-knell of our civilization. Money has become such a power as to make men lose sight of their souls and conscience and forget that they are a part of Universal Life. The greed of the world is the death of the world. The man whose mind is occupied with trying to get control of others that he may stand before the public as powerful and prosperous, that man is, from his soul's standpoint, in his death-throes.

We forget that a future awaits us and that there are more lives to be lived than this one. We ignore the spiritual will in man and that godlike part of our own nature which now more than ever should be brought into action; for this is the beginning of a cycle, a pivotal time in human history. Every age has its keynote. There was a period of political and religious despotism. This is one of inquiry, growth, and doubt. In proportion as we attain understanding of truth now, the evils that afflict the world will be eradicated as the cycle proceeds on its course. We are building the civilization of the future, and it is the first duty of the race today to see that the building is nobly done

It would be better for the peoples of the earth to sink into sleep and never see the sun again than to permit such another war as that we have recently suffered. I am thinking of the soldiers who die in battle, pitted man against man, and going out under the pressure of their bitter and bloodthirsty moods and the hatred, frenzy and madness of the conflict; and wondering to what condition the souls of them will gravitate; wondering and questioning because hatred begets hatred and brutality begets brutality, and though we had colossal intellects and all the wealth of the world we could not bend the divine laws of Nature to our desire.

I am thinking again of the effect of war on the generations that follow, and how something is lost out of the lives of all those born in war-time, so that monstrosities come into being and strange examples of human kind, a new race breathing the atmosphere of hatred, and embittered from birth and before birth—not a few of them here and there, but a whole generation of the unbalanced.

What we should remember is that the great power of the Divine Universe is in every human heart, even the most wretched and unfortunate; and it does not take a lifetime, it does not take a year, for a man to discover the God within himself. If he has the courage to face the issues he may find it in a moment of time. Let him, seeking truth, force the doors of his own Soul, and all human nature will be revealed to him. Let him find access there, and the desires and passions that have haunted him through life will disappear.

The light of the Soul shining in on the mind and coloring the life of a man—that is the glory of God; that is the glorification of Man; that is the establishment of everlasting peace. For each one of us is a universe in little, and each one has all the secrets of time within himself.

There is but one true and legitimate battlefield—the mind of Man, where the duality of our nature keeps us constantly at war, the only rightful war there is, the war of the god in us against the lower self. The kingdom of heaven is within, and no one is so far from the light and the truth that he cannot turn tomorrow and find it. We have come to be over-weighted with our exterior and worldly interests and have lost that natural human equilibrium by which we might live undisturbedly in the spiritual side of our nature, making our minds subservient to our real selves and using them as a means of service and growth; for we should regard the idea of adjusting national differences by brute force as an insult to the dignity of spiritual manhood.

All nations since the beginning have had their great successes and periods of high achievement followed by ages of spiritual and physical ignominy and the downward trend of their cycles. And we surely are in a cyclic decline and night-time now and not in the day and splendor of our season, for we do not understand in the least the real meaning of life, individual or national; our patriotism has coarsened abominably, and we reflect the coarse aspects of it on other nations, as they do the coarse aspects of theirs on us.

The Soul of a Nation, the living essence of its being, is the aggregation of its thoughts, feelings, actions, and ideals, backed by the divine quality of the god within. And to the degree that the people of any country nourish their national soul with thought of that spiritual and godlike kind, to that degree their country is protected, impregnable, beyond the reach of violation. Look at it rationally and you must see that this is the truth; but hug to your mind and heart the old contemptible fallacy that moral victories can be won by force, and you will go on being duped by foolishness and creating misery for yourself by sowing the seeds of war. Nation against nation, brother against brother and family against family, we shall always be at warfare as long as we place dependence on physical force, or on the selfish interest for the adjustment of those affairs which can only be settled by the spiritual side of man's nature.

None of the great world problems can be solved by mere cleverness. The man who depends solely on that can make nothing of any of them. In the direction of the mind our powers are always and necessarily limited; that is not the part of us which is immortal or without bounds. Therefore war cannot be abolished by argument or political intrigues or manipulations; but only by bringing to bear on our international questions the instincts and inspirations of that Divinity which stands now in the background of human consciousness—awaiting the summons of a humanity at last grown aware of the tremendous dignity of being human.

That man is still on his feet and can stand at all is proof enough of the essential divinity of man. Uncertain, changing, wandering, despairing, faltering; going down and constantly re-arising; his mind conceiving nothing of the depth and beauty and grandeur of the knowledge his Inner Self actually possesses, somehow he still endures. In the hell he has created for himself he still persists and is not extinguished. And what greater proof of his innner godhead could be imagined? Were he less than divine in essence and potentiality he would bow down his head and cease to be. The Soul knows. It has brought into this life memories of other and ancient lives and of old defeats and of victories. It abides forever in the light, choiring with the stars and the silences of God.

While the shadows are over us and the darkness still is about us we should turn our eyes to the east and realize that from within these death-cells of the body and mind we can look forth and see, faint as yet and far away perhaps, the promise of a new most glorious life for mankind. The Divine Laws are greater than the human laws. They are permanent and eternal and there is no change in them. Political systems do not touch them, nor sectarian influences corrupt. Right thought and action can lift us for the time being, always, on to the plane of the Soul. And when we are there we are raising the whole human race towards the level of its rights, possibilities, and spiritual heritage.

If but a few could grasp that central idea, if but a few could understand their duty in this matter, they would look into the future with broad and far vision. They would put away every fallacy and selfish aim in order to prepare for humanity a civilization in which war would be impossible. Their noble efforts would be directed towards welding, first their own countries, then the whole human family, into one impregnable unity. They could not, perhaps, put an end to war at once and forever—

karma will work itself out. But they would set their faces against the reign of brute force. They would see that there should be, as far as they could bring it about, a general recognition of the meaning and consequences of certain things we permit and even foster in our midst in peace-times and always: the cruelties, the upholdings of brute force as against decency and justice.

Why is not humanity aroused to its great need *before* disasters come? Why cannot we help each other *before* we are challenged by suffering or by war? Why cannot we move out beyond our limitations, in true compassion and with true love of justice, and ingrain into human life the spirit of brotherhood? Spiritual growth—that is the ideal. It is the only guarantee of permanent peace. Let us, by playing our part well, evoke the god of Peace, that it may brood over our fair land and breathe into the hearts of all a larger tolerance and a greater love for each other, for all nations and all people.

4

TO THE STUDENT: KEYNOTES ON THE PATH—I

First Thoughts Upon Waking

Practical Steps on the Way

Self-Directed Effort

The Middle Way

Last Thoughts Before Retiring

TO THE STUDENT:
KEYNOTES ON THE PATH—1

First Thoughts Upon Waking

When rising in the morning our first thought shall be, I shall make the day one of sunshine. I shall put into each duty no matter how small unselfish thought.

Aim to conduct your life as though each moment were the most precious in eternity, keeping an endless sacred festival in your heart and living all the year in the joy of service to humanity.

No day is commonplace if only you have eyes to see its splendor. With every nightfall a door is closed for the soul. Other lives and myriads of days will come to you, but never just the day that is ending, never that environment, those moments, those opportunities. They are gone, and long cycles of effort must be traversed before what they offered can return.

This very day you can make or mar your lives, and render them a blessing or a blasphemy. You can fill all the hours of it with such powerful affirmation of your hopes that they will become the world's hopes and the illumination of all life. No duty can come to you but will bring the possibility of doing kingly service.

Hence the importance of first thoughts upon waking. If one rises in the morning in a mood through which the Soul can express itself, one is at peace during the whole day. Remember how great is the creative power of the imagination. Build up with it, upon waking, a picture of hope and joy. Lay aside all that belongs to the lower self, and going up into the temple of the heart, dedicate the day to self-purification. Do this and you invite an invasion of the gods. But rise with the brain-mind dominant, and a day of perplexing difficulties awaits you.

Practical Steps on the Way

Electing difficult things while they are easy, and managing great things in their beginnings—this is the way, as the sages of antiquity have taught. The wise man takes account of small things and so never has any difficulty.

Do not worry; do not fear; do not think about results. Set plans come from the brain-mind, and in creative work that cannot be allowed to rule. There is a method of fashioning the life so that this will not be; then the brain-mind will keep its place as the servant, not the tormentor of the soul. It is something to think about when you get up in the morning and when you retire at night. It is very close to what I mean when I speak to you of trust in the Higher Law.

System, self-discipline, orderly habits:: these are the things that set the soul free and allow the mind to gather such breadth from its experiences that it comes to see itself a factor in the infinite harmony of law-governed manifested being. We have to learn to conserve our energies if we are to do our duty by the world.

How much we waste in a day for lack of this knowledge! How we talk ourselves to death on trifles, and die of chattering long before our time! What tearings, worryings, and confusion the poor brain-mind suffers where there has been no self-training in disciplined methods of thought!

Self-Directed Effort

There must be shadows, but we have the power to dispel them. When discouragement comes, and doubt and lack of faith, that is the time to bring imagination into play, to invoke the power of silence, to dig into the innner depths of one's own nature and discover there the beauty and grandeur of life, the glory of the Law. Had we no difficulties we should make no effort. Had we no temptations there would be no need for self-control. Had we no trials there would be nothing to call forth our patience and trust. Trust in what? In those universal Divine Laws that hold our life in their keeping. They are there, and all existence is governed by them. And therefore those who base their living on law and order are on the path of progress whether they know it or not; and those who live without discipline are retrogressing.

The secret of human life in its fulness is self-directed effort. Let man take the first step boldly in honest self-examination, with a daring that stops before nothing that may impede his path, and he will find very soon that he has the key to wisdom and to the power which redeems. Discovered through his own efforts, by the law of self-directed evolution, this key will open before him the chambers of the Self.

You ask, If I am divine by nature, why have I so many efforts to make, and so often unsuccessfully? The answer is that it is a part of the Scheme of Life. We are born into this world that we may grasp our opportunities to assert the nobler side of our consciousness. It is the law that man shall ever be changing, ever growing. The Soul's designs and the processes of its evolution move him, interiorly and otherwise, from condition to condition. The whole purupose of life is change, growth.

Some are burdened and aged by the consciousness of their failings. To give way thus is the sin against the Holy Ghost. Remember that two things cannot occupy the same place at the same time; and that of the two Companions, either the angel or the demon must win;

they cannot both be in possession. There is great danger for the one who in working towards his Higher Nature permits himself to dwell too long upon his failings. Indeed, to think of them at all is a mistake, and a sign that the courage is weakening.

The Middle Way

One of the greatest obstacles on the upward path is extremism: where the brain-mind has fashioned the way and the method and worked out its comparisons and put forward its severe criticisms of life. In such cases there is always a danger of the dogmatic attitude, and of finding oneself in a rut instead of swinging far out into the universal thought and moving forward along the broad road of spiritual effort. The strain that I know exists upon the body and mind of the extremist is terrible. Though no motive may be behind to do wrong or get away from the true, where there is that intense impulse to be doing something—to be getting a result without learning how, or bringing about some quick action contrary to one's better judgment—there at once the whole make up begins to deteriorate; and in weeks perhaps, or months, something may happen that will cause its complete undoing. This extremism becomes in a time a mania, a kind of insanity, and the brightest minds are often caught in the reaction.

Safety lies in keeping to middle lines. Do not look for phenomenal occurrences, nor expect any startling manifestation through or for yourself. The Divine Laws do not work that way, but in silence in the inmost part of our being. One must not take a yardstick to measure one's spiritual advancement. And remember that if you drop a single note in a melody the whole piece is spoiled. And so it is in our lives, the perfect harmony cannot exist if a false note is struck anywhere.

Rest within yourself. Do not depend upon another for your happiness. The moving away from the central source of one's inner life and from the duties near at hand has prevented spiritual growth in thousands, and wrecked thousands of lives. It is by endeavoring to do the great things rather than the small that we fail to find and follow the Law and to realize that our hearts are pulsating every moment in harmony with the finer forces of Nature and the inexpressible vibrations of Divine Life. It is ignorance of these facts that causes so much unrest in the nature of man.

A new life must come to humanity, else it will surely go down in darkness. We must be patient in the knowledge that we have within ourselves divine potentialities, and that to serve is to do what our souls long to do, so that all mankind may have glimpses of the blue of the future, and out beyond the shadows and horrors of the present behold the morning-star of a brighter day arisen.

For we plow the way for the human race. We cannot move along this path by ourselves, nor advance alone towards the Great Peace. We may not rest in the joy of being blessed, but by our devotion must bless the world.

Last Thoughts Before Retiring

At night it is helpful to go over the day in thought. It is the old neophyte way. You will suffer in noting lapses and omissions; but if your motive is pure and unselfish you will learn and pass on. And then will flash in upon you a sense of the nearness of the Higher Self, and ere you know it a new life will be born.

In sleep the soul is free, winging its way into new spaces, finer worlds of thought and feelings, evolving, growing, expanding. And it longs to carry you with it, the *you* beyond the prosaic life. The soul is within us—and yet it is not: there is a mystery here.

If you could only know what a companion the Higher Self can be! It is a Presence, a mystic Presence. The realization of it depends of course upon the degree of your evolution; but its companionship is so real, so wonderful, so royally supreme that once you have found it you never can lose it again. Just before retiring—that is the time.

We cannot reap the real benefit of sleep if we enter upon it negatively, in ignorance, carrying to bed with us our fretfulness and dislikes, despairs or hatreds. Let us end the day with more power of thought for self-conquest than we had at the beginning of the day. Let us close our eyes tonight with a clean conscience and with a feeling of generous love for all that breathes which is the best side of our natures. Let us seek more knowledge, more light, more strength in the silence of our last thoughts before retiring. To retire in the right spirit is to set aside the worries that have followed us during the day, to pass into sleep resting in the True, in a mood of utter trust in the wonderful Law and Mystery of Universal Life, and holding within a clearly defined aspiration for a better and sweeter tomorrow, and that we may wake fortified in the strength of the Soul's majesty.

Learn thus to conserve energy and the days and moments become ever more and more laden for you with beauty and meaning. At first all may be mystery and a conundrum; but hold the aspirations at heart and the great ideals ever before you, and the knowledge latent in you will open to your search, and you will take your position, and find in due time the peace that brings with it perfect understanding. Remember that these minds of ours that do so much thinking and cross-thinking and twisted thinking and lamentable thinking sometimes are but instruments for the Soul, the Master of all Music, to play upon.

Do well the smallest duty, and when the day is done there will be no regrets, no time wasted, then joy will come.

Let us not forget that we are gathered together at Lomaland for the purpose of serving humanity and bringing to it the knowledge that it needs; that this is not a commercial effort, nor simply an ordinary educational effort, but that *it is a spiritual effort in the highest sense;* and for that reason we must be spiritually endowed with those qualities that make for true nobility.

Think on these things in the silence. And remember that when a selfish or personal thought creeps in during silence, the door is shut and the Light cannot find its place; the soul is barred, and the day will bring little to you that will satisfy the better side of your nature.

5

TO THE STUDENT:
KEYNOTES ON THE PATH—2

The Sacredness of the Moment and the Day

The Beaming Thought

The Teacher's Work

The Mystic Path

TO THE STUDENT: KEYNOTES ON THE PATH–2

The Sacredness of the Moment and the Day

A pure, strong, unselfish thought, beaming in the mind, lifts the whole being to the heights of Light. From this point can be discerned, to a degree, the sacredness of the moment and the day.

Stand unfailingly on guard, the sentinel of your own inner nature, vigilant against the entry there of the least of the lurking foes about the doorway of the sanctum. Through that doorway goes and returns the soul, and it is your task to see that it is unimpeded in its freedom to act and to help.

A teacher is one who leads you to the Light; who shows you how to summon to your aid the help that lies hidden in the silences of life, in the silences of time and space, in the low, silent chambers of Duty. But you must do your part as student. Reflect!

Teacher and student are links in a great spiritual chain, extending from infinity to infinity, from past to future. Invisible and intangible, this nevertheless exists, a golden chain of spiritual life, a great Reality. As a link in this chain, man becomes both giver and receiver, passing on the torch of truth from hand to hand, from nation to nation, and from age to age.

Dare to be yourself, your greater Self! Dare to leap forward and be something you never before knew it was in you to be! Dare to move out and upward in the strength of your soul and find something new in your make-up. It is a critical time for everyone who aspires, for many things are in the balance. The need is for energy, aspiration, trust, and the power of the Spiritual Will. "The more one dares, the more he shall attain."

People copy each other too much; it is a universal human tendency. But you, as students of Theosophy, should not do so. Having evolved differently and through different experiences, each one of you has immense resources spiritually if you but draw upon them, so that you should learn to build your own atmosphere, as I so often say. Strike out on your own lines, not another's. In a word, have the courage to *be yourselves.*

The Beaming Thought

When the disciple begins consciously to deepen and broaden his life according to the highest law of his being, he must remember that confusion of ideas, behind which lies desire, will meet him at every step. The beaming thought as the Watcher and Master, recognized as such, becomes the helping power.

There is always the superb energy of eternity in the heart of one who does his best. If at the moment when this is felt the student would pause, reflect and meditate, he would find his way to the Light. The mysteries of his nature, his own Inner Self, would be revealed to him.

The Teacher's Work

Let it be remembered that the Teacher's work, the real work, *has naught to do with words written or spoken.* In the past, when vibratory forces were still understood, words were never used or looked for in the conveyance of the higher teachings. Let me make this clearer: Listen to the note of a bell resounding. Its vibrations get fainter and fainter, but though there comes at last a point, different for different people, when the sound is utterly lost for the outer ear, we know that the thrill is broadening out, and will forever go on doing so, into eternal and boundless space. And especially where the note is from a human voice it carries out with it a quality from the consciousness of him who sent it forth.

If you are in the right place, at the right time, and working in the right way, you have nothing in the universe to fear. And if you are following duty with that discrimination and resourcefulness that belongs to you as a soul, you *are* in the right place and working in the best possible way, however humble the duty may seem to be. "Nothing is great, nothing is small in the divine economy."

It is necessary, however, to discriminate between what is your duty and what is not; and the brain-mind cannot help you here. More than likely it will simply be in your way. You will have to seek refuge in the intuitional part of your nature, for intuition is the real, the mystic teacher. It is the voice of the soul in man.

Harmony is the key to all occult advance, and it is a knowledge of its laws and the relations of sound, number and color as applied and directed by the pupils that enables the Teacher to strike the higher tones and awake the spiritual vision.

The cry of my heart to you all is to be unto yourselves the Greater Selves. Never should you be half-hearted in any thought or act for the betterment of your fellows. Sound the depths of your own natures and restore the gods to their rightful place! Make humanity feel your strength! Heroically unite as warriors, called to serve in the darkest hours of the history of centuries! *This is our golden opportunity. We have earned the right.*

As to vigilance: how attentive we are to the material part of our lives in the sense of being vigilant! How much more attentive, as humanity goes, than to the spiritual! But as students of Theosophy we have a sacred duty: to study the duality of our nature and take a stand for vigilance in the inner life. Let us see that the help which goes out from us to another is help to the Higher Self. Vigilance on our part will give us power to render such help. Vigilance in spiritual things—that is the supreme need.

Climb! Ever keep climbing! The path winds upward, this wonderful path of self-mastery; but to the unselfish and courageous it is a path of victory and joy. Throw away the lower viewpoint, yes, throw it right out of your lives! You must unite for self-conquest. Then all other things will come! I have told you these things so often, but how can I help talking and talking, and pleading and pleading, and working and working? I do not want you to awaken when it is too late.

Difficult as it must be for you to believe what I say, yet it is true that the Kingdom of Heaven is nearer at hand than you can realize, and that all the storms, trials and sorrows that we see now raging in human life are but indications of the passing away of the old order of things. All that we have to do is to seize our opportunities, do faithfully our duties as they lie before us, ingrain in the very atmosphere in which we live the finer vibrations of the Higher Law, study and work, work and study.

Many of the greatest minds, in spite of all their knowledge, have come down in history as failures because they never found the inspiring light of the Soul. Study the lives of our writers, teachers, musicians, poets, inventors, and statesmen, and you will find how often, just when it seemed they were about to reach the heights, they faltered and failed, because they had been straining the brain-intellect—living wholly in that side of their nature and ignoring the sustaining spiritual power. The brain-mind is apt thus to exhaust itself in research and vain endeavor. We lose our way when we turn from the path of spiritual discovery.

Others, again, advance to a certain point and then hesitate and fall away because in the limitation of their lower mentality they expect results at a certain time: they must have their rewards, as they must have their dessert at dinner or they would lose their peace of mind. But the real seeker is indifferent to results; forgets himself altogether in the service of others; nurses in his nature the gentle and earnest spirit of justice, and treads the path carefully lest he should place one stumbling-block in the way of those who follow after.

The true doctrine is secret, hidden; not by the teacher, but in the very nature of the teaching itself, and to gain it, the student must enter by the only door which gives entrance, which is the living of the life. If the student will accept the primary truths of Theosophy and will seek to live according to them, every page and every line of *The Secret Doctrine* will have its message for him. But mere book study will avail little. Something more than that is required and demanded of the student of Theosophy; the full understanding of the teachings of all Theosophical works, and preeminently of *The Secret Doctrine,* is only possible as the life conforms to those teachings.

The student who seeks to fashion his life according to these teachings, finds himself more than an ephemeral spark of Being. He comes to realize that in very truth he is participant in an immortal drama, dating back for millions of years and stretching forward to heights and depths beyond the wildest dreams of poetic imagination. Yet he must learn too that the goal cannot be gained without effort, and that it depends upon himself to take part consciously in the glorious future that awaits the human race, and that conscious co-operation in the uplifting of the race is essential.

Wisdom comes not from the multiplication of spoken or written instruction; what you have is enough to last you a thousand years. Wisdom comes from the performance of duty and in the Silence, and only the Silence expresses it. It will come in the living of the pledge you have taken to your Higher Selves, illuminating all you have been taught or may learn; strengthening, till at last you become invulnerable, every weak place in your nature; answering one by one, the very deepest problems of your life, solving all mysteries, and bringing into your lives the Light and Harmony of the Great Lodge, which is the Heart of the World.

The Mystic Path

The mystic is one who lives ever in the consciousness of his Divinity. He senses intuitively the divine life in all things. He sees within the outer, which is fleeting and perishable, an Inner which is imperishable and eternal.

The path of the mystic is a secret path, in a sense, and a silent and wonderful path. Yet it is open to all, and is so simple and so near at hand that many who long to tread it yet turn away from it thinking it to be something else.

He in whom the soul is ever active, ever urging to compassionate thought and deed, he is the true mystic, and to him Theosophy is no system of sterile thought but a light, a teacher, a companion, ever calling to compassionate action, ever urging to higher things.

A vow is an action rising like a star high above the level of the common deeds of life. It is a witness that the outer man at that moment realized its union with the inner, and the purpose of its existence, registering a great resolve to become one with the 'Father in Heaven'. At that moment the radiant Path of Light is seen with the eye of pure vision, the disciple is reborn, the old life is left behind, he enters a new way. For a moment he feels the touch of a guiding hand ever stretched out to him from the inner chamber. For a moment his ear catches the harmonies of the soul.

All this and more is the experience of those who make this vow with their whole hearts; and as they constantly renew it, and constantly renew their endeavor, the harmonies come again and again, and the clear Path is once more beheld. They carry the inspiration into outer life, and energize with it their common duties, high and low; gain from it strength for self-sacrifice, and thus bringing the inner into the outer, pouring forth in deeds that wine of Divine Life of which they have learned to partake, they achieve, little by little, the harmony of perfect life. Each effort carves the path of the next, and in no long time one single moment's silence will bring forth to the disciple's aid the strength of his soul.

Take, if only a few moments for meditation, on rising and before sleeping; renew your resolve; seek union with your higher nature; review the thoughts, acts, failures and opportunities of the day just ended. No one is so busy that he cannot give five minutes night and morning to this; no one too tired, for it will give inner strength and refreshment both to mind and body. Yet do not let meditation end with this. True meditation is for all the hours. Do every act as an intent and loving service of the Divine Self of the World, putting your best into it in that way.

Thus living, your struggles will gradually end, one by one, in victory. Success does not come without effort, without long and often repeated efforts, but the intensity and imposed necessity of the struggle, your very desire to make the effort, show you that there is already a living power within your heart that demands and will reward beyond all conception your strong and unfaltering service. Be hopeful, then, not despairing. With each morning's awakening try to live through the day in harmony with the Higher Self. 'TRY' is the battle-cry taught by the Teachers to each pupil. Naught else is expected of you. One who does his best does all that can be asked.

Fear nothing, for every renewed effort raises all former failures into lessons, all sins into experiences. Understand me when I say that in the light of renewed effort the karma of all your past alters; it no longer threatens; it passes from the plane of penalty before the soul's eye up to that of tuition. It stands as a monument, a reminder of past weakness and a warning against future failure.

So fear nothing for yourself. You are behind the shield of your reborn endeavor, though you have failed a hundred times. Try slowly to make it your motive for fidelity that others may be faithful. Fear only to fail in your duty to others, and even then let your fear be for them, not for yourself. Not for thousands of years have the opposing forces been so accentuated. Not one of you can remain neutral. If you think you can and seek to do so, in reality you are adding your powers to the forces of darkness and lending your strength to the forces of evil. The cry has gone out to each, and each must choose. This is your opportunity.

Will you have it recorded that your vow was of the lips or of the heart? You have studied and thought, many of you long and faithfully. Bring forth the fruit of this now as action, for the hour has struck. Humanity calls for aid. Who of you has the strength, the will, to go forward? To them I call, and upon them already is the flush and the Light of the Victory beyond conception.

6

WHY I AM A THEOSOPHIST

What is Theosophy?

A Broader Conception of Deity

The Teaching of Reincarnation—Another Chance

Right Thoughts About Karma

Death and Rebirth

WHY I AM A THEOSOPHIST

What is Theosophy?

Theosophy was once the universal religion of mankind, and it is destined to be the universal religion of the future. Even now its great principles are permeating thought and action everywhere, and everywhere the most advanced minds are looking forward to the ideal of a universal religion as humanity's one hope. Theosophy is the essence of all religions. It satisfies the intellect; it is logical, scientific and clear; and it steals into the heart with its message of brotherliness and compassion like the aroma of a flower, like the tender breath of a mother's love.

The teachings of Theosophy alone can bring hope to poor, storm-tossed humanity. This I affirm, and we have but to observe the general trend of human thought and effort to establish this as a fact. Antiquated theories of religion and life are being discredited, long settled beliefs and customs are being abandoned, and there has risen in the world a great compelling force which is demonstrating the poverty of man's religious life.

Materialism and the merely intellectual view have carried man out upon a sea of unrest and dissatisfaction, while the real man, the Divine Man, has been ignored. As a result, the finer knowledge—which is right at hand if we could but perceive it, for it lies in the very being of man himself—is inactive and obscured, so that it is difficult even for thinking men and women to find their moorings. It is this very condition, however, that will finally open man's eyes to the power and beneficence of Theosophy, and to the fact that it holds the key to knowledge which he seeks.

Theosophy is as old as the hills, and all the world-religions are based on its teachings, although only a minority now are familiar with them. It is not superstition nor speculation; not dogmatism nor blind faith; nor yet miraculous. It comes to humanity like an old traveler who has trodden all the highways of experience; and having achieved after long journeying a full understanding of life, returns to the place from which he started, that he may bring to those who still dwell there the saving knowledge of the God within Man, and of man's power to advance and to overcome, which is what evolution means.

Superficial examination of its teachings will avail nothing. As none could become a musician by mere study of the theory of music, so none can come to a full understanding of Theosophy by reading of it only. In both cases, practice is needed: one must live the life if one would know the Law.

Think of Theosophy not so much as a body of philosophic or other teaching, but as the highest law of conduct, which is the enacted expression of divine love or compassion.

Theosophy will bring something to you that can never pass away: the consciousness of your divine, your inner Self; a conviction of your inherent power to conserve your energy along the highest spiritual lines. For man cannot find his true place in the great scheme of human life until he has ennobled and enriched his nature with the consciousness of his divinity. That is what Theosophy means. That is its message.

We consider the Theosophical Movement the most serious movement of the age. It offers to every human soul the key to the real meaning and purpose of life. It teaches man whence he came, whither he goes. It explains something at least of the divine laws governing the universe.

The wisdom-religion of Theosophy is countless thousands of years older than Christianity. Its teachings are available, and all one has to do is to turn toward them as he would to the sun. One has not to give up any truths that he already has in his religious views. Theosophy accepts the essential teachings of all religions. The actual teachings of Jesus himself are pure Theosophy. He had no church, he had no creed, and he taught us to love one another. And not until men can love one another, as he was in himself an example of a man truly capable of loving, can they begin to know what it is to be a Theosophist, or what human life means.

Theosophy presents none of the gruesome religious pictures that we were taught in our childhood. Man is not told that he was 'born in sin,' or that 'hell' will be his eternal abiding-place if he does wrong. Theosophy says that the world belongs to humanity, that the soul of man is eternal; that his destiny in a sense is as fixed as the stars, if he will turn his face towards the light, if he will respond to that indescribable, pulsating something, that spiritual urge in his heart.

No man living, no matter how he has failed, has ever completely lost touch with that certain quality of tenderness and gentleness and nobility, which is the eternal part of him, though it may seem lost; and if he does not find it today, he may find it tomorrow. So the hope, the grandeur, the superb optimism of the psychology of true Theosophy is just what the nations need today.

This does not mean that the churches should disappear, nor that the pulpits should be closed; but it does mean that every human being shall have the right to think for himself and to give his own soul a chance to live. I can conceive that your preachers, great as some of them are, good as many of them are, would find in Theosophy the key to the solution of their problems. It never can be taken away from them; and then they will begin to present to the human mind a grander conception of deity—Impersonal, Infinite, Unknowable, All-Loving, All-Just. This is what every man must seek.

In looking over the condition of the world today, and going back to the time of Christ and the early Fathers who were laying the foundation of the Christian church, by careful study we shall find that what I call the retrogression of the church began in about the second century of the Christian era. Jesus himself preached a divinely beautiful teaching, without dogma, creed, or church.

We find also that in Rome and in Greece and in Alexandria there were three schools of purely pagan religious thought flourishing when Christianity began. That word *pagan* used to frighten me when I saw the books in our library telling dreadful things about the pagans. But the Theosophist who studies comparative religion and who goes far back into ancient history cannot help but realize that the majority of those following the pagan religions, at least several centuries before Christ, were leading a very true life, and many of their teachings were beautiful and lofty.

There are cycles of time referred to, I think, by Plato, who lived about four hundred years before Christ, cycles in which all that was true and beautiful was on the upward path and the minds of men were fertile and ready for spiritual truths. Then there are other cycles which Plato said a great deal about and which we Theosophists also explain in our books, periods when the whole tendency of men's minds was unspiritual and downwards. I think if we study very closely we shall find that we can liken the present time to the time I referred to as the early retrogression in spiritual thought.

To make my position very clear I must remind my readers that a true Theosophist has no disposition to destroy anything that is good, but always seeks to preserve all that is of real value. Theosophy is the parent of all religions, and Theosophy recognizes the essential spiritual teachings in all the different religious forms. I find that the Pagans belonging to the three schools I have spoken of, the Stoics, the Neo-Platonists, and the Neo-Pythagoreans, taught many of the great teachings of the Ancient Wisdom, and that the few essential spiritual doctrines of the Christian church today are really derived from these three schools. But from the second century of the Christian era we have dogmas and creeds taking the place of the simple teachings of Jesus which were easily understood by all; and it is the dogmas and creeds that Theosophy does not recognize and accept.

In the first place the Church began at about that time to instill into the minds of the followers of Christianity the dogma that they were born in sin. I never lose an opportunity to say that Theosophists cannot accept this doctrine. To accept the teaching of original sin is to limit the power of Deity. How can we accept the idea that the Omnipresent, the Unknowable, the All-Loving, All-Compassionate Deity could place humanity in a position with no choice in coming into life, and then mark it as being born in sin?

I do not presume to say that this dogma was introduced with any evil intention. I know nothing about the states of mind of those who organized and introduced it. They may have had the same view as the severe father of Puritan days, *spare the rod and spoil the child.* But the tendency of the doctrine was certainly to intimidate the human mind. And we cannot rise to the position of true self-respect that should be ours until we eliminate that idea from our minds. The moment we can take this step we can throw ourselves, so to say, towards the Infinite, resting in a beautiful and unselfish trust. Then we shall have enlightenment; then will come the knowledge that every man should have in order to guide and direct his life spiritually.

Amid the jangling of creeds and the blind groping of scientific theories, Theosophy alone stands unmoved, the Wisdom-Religion of the ages; not as a theory, not as a supposition or a mere working hypothesis, but as a body of teaching that has been handed down throughout the whole life-history of man, and whose statements have been verified by the Sages of all times. Like a great beacon it sheds its light over heartsick humanity which cries out in the darkness of its despair, asking ever Why? Why? Why all this awful suffering, why the perplexities, the injustices of life?—asking questions regarding man, his origin, his destiny, and the purpose of life: the Riddle of the Universe.

The mission of Theosophy is to set aside errors, misconceptions, unbrotherliness and intolerance, and put love and trust, right action and the sweetness of truth, in their place. Its mission is to spread new ideas throughout the world for the benefit of those who most need them; to release the mind of man from prejudice and fear, and human life from its digressions. Its mission is to bring the whole human family up to a standard of spiritual foresight, discrimination, intuition, right thought and right action, and with a new and diviner conception of justice and of love. If men and women could work together as one great universal body towards this end they would be creators of a new order of ages, a Universal Religion verily—a true Brotherhood of Man.

But alas, unbrotherliness is the insanity of the age. It menaces, to no small degree, the progress of our civilization. Its power cannot be broken or destroyed until man has had ingrained into his heart and mind the fact that he is divine in nature, until he realizes that he possesses the immortal potentiality of good, that true freedom exists only where the Higher Law holds in subjection the lower nature.

Not until he seeks to gain the ascendency over his lower nature can man do his highest duty to his fellow-men, or be a brother in the truest sense of the word, or live in the freedom of Freedom.

Let us hope with that grander hope of the soul, the energy of right action, that the day is not far distant when the great sweeping force of Love—of true brotherliness, shall encompass humanity, when the knowledge of right living shall be in the grasp of all, and shall be lived in the truest sense of the word, when children shall be conceived and educated in the atmosphere of purest thought and grander action. Then and not until then shall humanity commence to build the solid foundations of a golden age.

Universal Brotherhood has no creeds or dogmas. It is built on the basis of common sense. It teaches that man is divine, that the soul of man is imperishable, and that Brotherhood is a fact in Nature, and consequently takes in all humanity.

And this is really the keynote—the recognition of the soul in all men, whether they be black or white, despairing or hopeful. It is in all, even though our civilization, our desires, our reason may seem to choke it; even though science in its blindness may not see it. Yet it stands majestic, the core and heart of each man's life, the dictator of his being, the director of his destiny.

A Theosophist makes no attempt to proseletize or convert. Our philosophy declares that any attempt to force others to accept our thought or our views is an injustice to their true nature, their deeper self. We do not intimidate or discourage, nor do we implant fear. But we do appeal, we do plead, and we do try by the example of our lives to show to others the beauty of Theosophy as a living power.

A Broader Conception of Deity

Let me carry you in thought, if possible, to a broader conception of Deity—the Absolute, the Supreme, nay more, the Omnipresent Divine Essence in everything visible and invisible. He who is inspired by this broad conception would soon find himself outgrowing the old limitations of the belief in a personal God. He would begin to realize that there are invisible laws so close at hand, touching all life, that if man could only understand them, he could rise in his strength and become, without struggle, without strenuous effort, without fear or suffering, free from the bondage and thraldom of the old theological ideas that have been taught to us during recent ages. I often wonder if the progressive minds of the age realize the strong psychological power of the old dogmas which seem to be teeming in our very blood. Truly we are the progeny of the ignorance of the past, and we have much to learn ere we can lift the burdens from our fellow-men.

Let us take this idea of Deity. Deity pervades the whole Universe: it is impersonal, unknowable, no matter how near we may draw to the light of it. It is the absolute, the Goal which we climb towards forever, forever learning and growing in the will and power to serve; forever acquiring new and grander ideals of That towards which we climb.

Think of the great Supreme Source of Life that holds the stars in their places, that orders nature and its wonderful mysteries, that gives to mother and father the sacred privilege of parenthood. Think of these and then tell me who can limit the Universal, Supreme Deity! Who can attempt to limit human life? At your best moments, at your silent moments, when either by despair or joy you have been moved to a state of contemplation, of analysis, of questioning, of yearning, think a moment, have you not sometimes almost felt the touch of this divine power in your longings and in your aspirations? Think what it would be if the human mind could be ever conscious of the fact that man is part of the great, central, spiritual life, a ray of the Supreme!

He who understands this, knows what is the dignity of Man; and that the religion which alone will fitly correspond to our innate religious nature will be a universal system of human brotherhood based on the knowledge that we are essentially divine; a system that will warm our hearts with the knowledge that there is nothing outside ourselves that can save or damn us; that it is we ourselves who alone must and can work out our own salvation.

It is impossible to gage the significance of the present time or to realize what is in store for humanity during the next hundred years, merely from our own experience and from recorded history. For this is no ordinary time; it is not simply the culminating point of the past hundred years, but of thousands of years. The night of centuries has passed, and with the new dawn comes the return of memories and powers and possibilities of an age long past.

The Teaching of Reincarnation—Another Chance

There are three outstanding principles of Theosophy which should never be forgotten. They are the doctrines of karma, of reincarnation, and of the actuality of human perfectability. In regard to this last doctrine we have not only the belief, but the absolute knowledge, that man can attain through self-devised efforts to such a high degree of evolution that for any one period he may be said to have reached a state of relative perfection, but with the possibility of attaining a still larger and profounder state of development in future evolutionary periods.

How trivial human existence is when viewed from the standpoint of only one life-time on earth! Why, what can the man with even the greatest aspirations really do or work out in these few years that he passes here in this school of experience of one lifetime? But Theosophy says that he has another chance in another life, and after that other chances in other lives. Why, even Nature teaches us this lesson of going to sleep in its wintry rest and reawakening in the spring.

Man is immortal in his soul-life. When the physical body dies, when man throws off this garment of flesh, the immortal soul, the man himself, that which is a part of this Universal Scheme, goes on. It does not go to a point in space; it does not stand still; it has within itself growing and developing qualities—the potential qualities of Divinity—and consequently the soul goes on. It carries man into a condition too divinely beautiful to describe, but whatever the condition, it is not sleep in the sense of inertia. It sleeps in activity, and when according to natural law it has completed its rest, its education, its development, it returns to earth to begin again—not on the same lines as before, but taking the knowledge and the experience of the past life and applying them to growth and advancement in the new.

Many who have abandoned belief in a personal god and the other vanities and subtleties of sectarian metaphysics, and are thinking seriously, in the depression the unrest of the age is causing in them, of life and its many problems, have found in the teaching of Reincarnation that which makes clear the meaning of it all. For here is explanation of the differences of human fortune, so that they cease to seem unjust and intolerable; and here Man is revealed in the splendor of his native godhood, a traveler through eternity, moving from life to life, gaining by experience after experience that knowledge which will make of him at last the Ideal, the Perfect Man.

We are of the family of the Eternal. We are the highest expressions that we know of of Universal Deity. Are we to think that the experience to which we have a right can be gained in the few score fleeting years of a single lifetime, before these bodies of ours cease to be useful and drop away following the laws of physical life and return to the storehouse of Nature? The material things have their place; but the essential and everlasting things are in the eternal self. They are the attributes and faculties of the Soul. And these are what we are here to develop, working in harmony with the mighty and compassionate heart of Nature.

No matter how noble a man's life may have been, is it possible to think of it as having reached that sublimity of perfection in one single lifetime that would find its true expression in an eternity of bliss? How much more reasonable to believe that we live again and again, traveling the path of the ages with opportunity after opportunity recurring always, than to imagine ourselves the poor creatures of a single life, created at our birth out of nothing, and at death to be relegated to an eternal heaven or an unending hell, in neither of which progress is possible, nor opportunities are to be found, nor any goal lies ahead, nor hope exists for inspiration and incentive!

To what purpose are the ideals we cherish unspoken, the secret, noble, and unfulfilled aspirations, the questions we put to life, and to which life—our present life—makes no answer? To what end are the agonies and despairs, the unrest and intense longing to be so much more than we can ever attain to being, now, before death takes us? Were they born in a day, these thoughts of ours that stir us sometimes almost to the point of revelation? Were they fashioned of the experience we have gathered in the few years since our bodies were born? Their word to us is always that we are greater than we seem, that there are no limits to the power of the Soul, that though our understanding of this universe will go on increasing forever and ever, we shall never attain a dead finality of understanding, that we have all eternity in which to work out the magnificence of the Law, and that there is no break in the everlasting continuity; that one may falter today and fail, but tomorrow brings another chance; that we live many lives, again and again the same in essence though different in aspect—we Immortal Beings, natives of Eternity made subject here to mortality and time.

Thus Reincarnation gives us room and time to grow, as Nature provides soil and season for the flowers—to grow and to learn what life and the world can teach us, and to acquire use of the godlike qualities of our inner selves and the light hidden within the Soul of Man which alone can illumine the path we must tread and enable us to solve the stern and awful problems, the pathetic problems, life so unceasingly sets before us, and to know its unspeakable beauties as well.

We advance from age to age and from heights to greater heights forever. Understanding this, the old become young again in spirit, and the young look out on the world with a new joy. The days are long and the path is wide. Go forward, then, with far-seeing hope and trust, towards the Great Ultimate!

Right Thoughts About Karma

Great care is needed that you should have right thoughts about Karma. The word means *action.* In its widest sense it is that great law of Nature recognized by all as the law of cause and effect, not only on the physical plane but on the mental and spiritual planes as well. H. P. Blavatsky speaks of it as "the *Ultimate Law* of the Universe, the source, origin and fount of all other laws which exist throughout nature."

But do not make the common mistake to think that Karma brings only evil or painful results. Karma is the harvest of the good seed you have sown as well as the tares or weeds. Nor should you fall into the common error of thinking that Karma must always be immediate in its action. The harvest both of good and evil may be long delayed, though it is always certain, for "Tomorrow thou shalt reap, or after many days."

Those of you who love your Bible will find frequent references to Karma, though it is not called by that name. The words are familiar to you, "Be not deceived, God is not mocked, for whatsoever a man soweth *that* shall he also reap."

Karma is a beneficent law. What sort of a universe would it be if we could not trust in the natural connection between cause and effect? But even more than that, Karma is that divinely wise and just law which "moves to good", and tends to bring order out of chaos, good out of evil, joy out of pain. I find it strange that while some believe Karma rules in the physical world they do not believe or trust Karma in the moral world. We know we shall burn our hand if we put it in the fire, and therefore we trust the law and avoid the fire. But do we know or believe with equal certainty that truth, honesty, purity have their karma, and that lies, dishonesty, impurity have also theirs? The entire moral color of the world would change if men believed in Karma in the moral realm as firmly as they believe in its action in the physical. Can you not see why it was that one of the great Teachers declared that Karma and Reincarnation are the two great truths which the world specially needs for its salvation!

Let us remember we are today the sum of our yesterdays. Karma is no more Fate than the harvest of the seed we have sown. Learn to meet your Karma with equal-mindedness. Learn from it those lessons which it teaches and which both enlighten and bless. Throw aside that negative, hopeless condition which some manifest who say, Oh, it is my Karma; I must submit; I can do nothing! True, we must reap what we ourselves have sown; but Present and Future are not a mere reproduction of Past, or life would be an endless treadmill and progress impossible. The inner divine Self can daily and hourly exert an inherent, direct power to modify the results of the past. We can rise upon our past, making even our vices, when placed beneath our feet, stepping-stones to higher things.

Another view of Karma which is as false as the worn-out orthodox notion of hell is that which makes one say—perhaps for one he may dislike or may have injured—Leave him to his own Karma! That is wrong and hypocritical. To indulge in that attitude hardens the heart and kills out compassion. Those who seek to excuse themselves from helping the needy by saying "It would interfere with his karma" are not living rightly. They cannot realize the truth of Universal Brotherhood; they cannot truly believe that all are parts of a great whole and that one member of the body cannot suffer without the other members also suffering.

And remember this also. Because mistakes and misdeeds bring suffering, it does not follow that all suffering is caused by sin and error. If this were so then the Helpers of Humanity, who have been great sufferers, would be great sinners. The mother in helping her sick child suffers. The nurse in the fever hospital suffers. And the Great Ones who have traveled the path we seek to tread and out of their knowledge and compassion help us, also suffer. They suffer "in holding back with strong hands the heavy Karma of the world" through coming close to those they would help. But in that suffering there is triumphant joy in helping those who are weak and needy. Helping and sharing is indeed the basic law of the universe.

Death and Rebirth

Just as one life is not enough to satisfy man's highest hopes so is there another beautiful idea that has made me a Theosophist. It is the theosophical idea of death or rebirth. As a child my nurse taught me about a punishing God and about His Satanic Majesty, the Devil, It made me unhappy. I did not want anything in my religion or my life that would hold up before me a picture of fear. So I perceived at an early age that fear is the result of a limited view of life, that is all. The only thing to be afraid of is doing wrong. No other fears should have place in the life of man. For his own inner nature, his own higher nature, should show him that if he has sorrow, somewhere along the path there has been a cause for it. If somebody has treated him unjustly, he can explain it. If he is persecuted he can keep on with his work and face his enemies and conquer in the end. Why? Because he has the consciousness of not being as he has been represented to be. And so he pursues his way in full confidence.

In our theosophical belief when death comes the soul is released. The body goes to the earth. The passions, the weaknesses, the mistakes, and the sorrowful memories go with the body. But the soul, the eternally living part of our divine nature, passes on to another life, through the law of evolution.

Why do we not trust these immutable Laws? Simply because our views are limited. We pay little attention to the blessings that have been given us. We half-live from day to day. We struggle. We doubt. We have half-faith. And when we die, we die in the shadows because we are not certain of the future. But Theosophy brings home to man the consciousness of his essential divinity. It declares there is no limit to the love of the Divine. There is no limit to the possibilities of man. I am convinced that there is but one religion, and that is the Universal Religion, Theosophy.

Theosophy shows the glory and richness of what we call death, and how pitiful a thing it is that we should mourn for the dead, of whose immortality our very memory of them is a token, and that we shall meet them again.

We are outgrowing fast—evolution is helping us to outgrow—the old idea of a personal God; and with it must throw away the concept that a man's soul enters this world newly created from such a deity's hands. We grow towards knowledge that in the great economy of Nature a soul born here comes as a guest out of far realms in eternity, a guest of whose past we know nothing but that it has lived through the ages and abides here for awhile, and goes.

Whither? When we brood on that which is immortal in ourselves the answer comes back to us out of the living Silence, and we know that life is eternal, and death but a stepping forth into larger fields of life. When one we love is so released we are given opportunity to realize the majesty of the Higher Law, whose manifestation then is so close to us; and to turn our thoughts from the impermanent to the permanent, and away from all that holds us to our limitations.

There is indeed that in us which is mortal and has no place in the eternity of things. It belongs to this present life only, and must be thrown aside at last. But deep in our hearts we know that we are deathless, and that within us are the starry light and the wonderful places where truth abides. The external and fascinating attachments which we hug most dearly will fade away, but this bright and inward knowledge will never dessert us.

None should be so immersed in his personal concerns

as to lose sight of the time when he, too, must take his place in the Silence. Many, working against themselves, spend two thirds of their time seeking knowledge from this writer or that, and following fads and fallacies and absurd teachings; so that when the hour of death comes they are wholly unprepared for the new life Nature has in store for them.

Indeed, we should live, I think, twice as long as we do could we but get rid of the fear of death and perceive that it is a new birth, and that it is life, and realize that it is joy; beyond the present moment and beyond the end of our days looking forward to vast possibilities and an endless succession of opportunities; aware that one life is not enough, that the soul could do justice neither to itself nor to the universal plan without the large experience of many.

We might awake each morning in such self-forgetfulness that were death to visit us at noonday we should accept it with as much gladness as we do the smiles of the sun. On rising and before sleep, and indeed through all our duties in the daytime, we could hold to the idea that the Higher Laws exist, that they brought us into life and will take us out of it in a way more merciful than we with all our planning could devise; and we could go forth at last with broad vision and deathless trust, feeling only the beneficent glory of the change. For though a man die even in the depths of degradation that Compassionate Law that is a part of our natures takes command at the passing. And whatever the mistakes may have been, or the ignorance or the sorrow, there is an hour or a moment of glorious victory in what to our eyes seems the tragedy of death. It comes to the dying man when he feels that he is being released, and stepping forth into the unknown, knows that he goes not unprotected, not without companionship; for it is the Knower, it is the Great Warrior, it is the Eternal Self that is there with him. And the Soul arises in the power of its divinity and knows no fear nor pain. When the eyes were closed and the lips silenced, I have seen the light and beauty of a great illumination on the sweet faces of the dead.

Though seemingly remote and unknowable, the Higher Law with resistless force guides man to the destiny he has carved for himself. As Nature works in her unseen processes, so does the Soul, set free. Having gone forth, it seeks its own: not at some point in space as the theologians teach, but in a condition in which, freed from the body, it may gain strength and knowledge; recalling in the silence its old victories until, having learned the lessons they teach, it may put forth towards fresh experience and take up anew a tenement of the flesh.

When we consider the mercy that comes to our rescue—cares for us in spite of ourselves—liberates the Real Self in us, and allows it to move into the new life, we can soar above our worldly interests and enter into loftier activities of thought, realizing what a marvelous experience this change must be that brings illumination to the disprisoned soul. We sorrow at a death and the tears come only because we do not see the grander vistas of life but have fashioned our minds in the dogmatism of the ages and let the habit of our ancestors rule us.

When a soul separates itself from the body it does not immediately pass on. Its old surroundings hold it for a while. It is aware of our pangs of bereavement; our mourning hinders its escape. The great onward march is before it. It is not what we knew here, but greater. All the limitations were from the brain-mind, which is dead. It would be forging upward, advancing and expanding. We do it wrong to be hampering its flight. We should let it go free as the birds in the air, free as the Law intended it should be. We should part with our loved ones without grief; with confidence, as though they were but going on a journey, watchful lest we drop our minds into a belief that there is death, when it is only a rebirth that has occurred. Let our mental pictures be the reverse of sorrowful, bright with hope and music, beautiful with love and flowers—and I can almost see the departing soul sending back a benediction as it passes into the world of Light.

The small mind may say, *I have had more than enough of life, I do not want to live again.* But this is no better than cowardice and the attitude of the man who would sit down and neglect his duties and responsibilities and forget them. Belief in reincarnation inspires us to stand on our feet and hold our shoulders back and our heads high in superb confidence, because of the Divinity of Man.

To come into a nearness to eternal things we must have life after life, experience on experience. We must have known all sorrow and heart-ache, all agony and despair. It is the pressure of these things that is bringing us slowly to our own, so that we may find within our hearts at last the knowledge that passeth understanding, the peace that shall abide with us by night and in the daytime, through all eternity, and no less in our griefs than in our joys.

There is no such thing as chance. Divine Law governs us. The ills a man causes he can cure, and the seeds of the conditions that oppress us now were sown by us in former lives. You may be suffering and in ill health, and have in memory no time when in this life you set in motion the currents of physical decay and prepared for yourself the trials you are undergoing. Is there no bright promise for you? Can you not find new strength to meet life each morning in the knowledge that as you are reaping that which you have sown so you shall reap that which now you are sowing?

Were a man to die tomorrow in the belief even that we live but this once, when death had come he would find himself enligtened; for to the soul in its passing, when the lips are already mute and the mind seems unconscious, a sure and certain knowledge comes. It understands how unreal the life just past has been, and that all its activities here were unfinished business. Memory for awhile is vivid and strong. Spiritual light is thrown upon the path ahead. Revelations come of what might have been and what yet is to attain, and the soul cries out for a larger opportunity, that in the light of the experience it has gained it may begin again, correct old mistakes, make fresh efforts, build anew, and build with understanding. And with the aspiration comes the answer: in the Divine Economy endless opportunities are accorded.

Let us move out then into the light of thought and trust life confidently. Let us rest in the knowledge that the Law is mercy, and it shall show us in our waking and our sleeping moments that the old idea of death is a farce, and that what seemed a monster waiting to destroy us is a benediction under the laws of God and the working of our destiny.

Theosophists are striving to attract the attention of humanity to a consciousness of the essential divinity of man. Our purpose is not to convert people. It is not to persuade them to join the Universal Brotherhood and Theosophical Society. It is not to remind them of their sins and their mistakes, but to show humanity that there is an open door to the path of peace and of success—moral and spiritual success. That door can be found through the study of Theosophy and its application in daily life. If one lives a true, noble, unselfish, clean, intelligent life, he is a Theosophist. It was through the experiences which I had in helping the needy and the discouraged, and the study of human nature that this awakened in me, that I found myself closely in harmony with the teachings of the Divine Wisdom, Theosophy. That is why I am a Theosophist.

7

BASIC PRINCIPLES OF TRUE EDUCATION

The Perfect Balance of All the Faculties

Music—and the Harmony Within

Drama, Its Rightful Place

The Mystery-Drama

BASIC PRINCIPLES OF TRUE EDUCATION

The Perfect Balance of All the Faculties

I realized many years ago that something was vitally wrong with all our scheme of things—with our conventions, our reformatory efforts, our charities. In the very shadow of the churches I saw vice and suffering and want. Worse still, everywhere I saw people moving along the even tenor of their ways, blissfully oblivious or frankly indifferent.

Never could I reconcile myself to such a bland acceptance of things. I must at least try to ameliorate conditions. I saw hardship as a result of vice, and vice as the outcome of hardship. I realized that all of our systems of helpfulness were totally backhanded. We dealt then, as most people deal now, with effects rather than causes. *After* the damage is done we attempt to repair. What I wanted to do was *to prevent*—to prevent the damage being done. The world was already fairly well equipped with havens for the beaten and the fallen. I wanted to evolve an institution that would take humanity in hand *before* it was worsted in the struggle of life.

The term education has a much wider significance at the Raja Yoga School at Point Loma than is usually given it. The basis of this education is the essential divinity of man, and the necessity for transmuting everything in his nature which is not divine. To do this no part can be neglected, and the physical nature must share to the full in the care and attention which are required. Neither can the most assiduous training of the intellect be passed over; it must be made subservient, however, to the forces of the heart. The intellect must be the servant, not the master, if order and equilibrium are to be attained.

The truest and grandest thing of all as regards education is to attract the mind of the child to the fact that the immortal Self is ever seeking to bring the whole being into a state of perfection. The real secret of the Raja-Yoga system is rather to evolve the child's character than to overtax the child's mind. It is to bring *out* rather than to bring *to* the faculties of the child. The grander part is from within.

Raja-Yoga is an ancient term meaning simply 'royal' or 'kingly union'. I selected it as best expressing the aim and object of true education, namely, the perfect balance of all the faculties, physical, mental and spiritual—in a word, *character*.

Seeing that the children of today will be the men and women of the future, the great importance of this work surely cannot be over-estimated. Only by wise teaching, by training in self-reliance, self-discipline, concentration, and a recognition of the power of silence, can the lower qualities of the nature be overcome and the higher developed, so that the children who are brought in touch with this Movement shall in their turn become practical workers for humanity. One of the great objects must be to bring home to their minds the old, old teaching that they are Immortal Souls, not divorced from beneficent nature, but in deed and truth a part of it.

Our work is distinctively international, and this has its effect upon the children. Students come here, both young and old, from all parts of the world, and each is encouraged to be, in the deeper sense, a national expression, standing for all that is best and highest in his own national life. Children are taught to regard themselves as integral and responsible parts of the nation to which they belong. They are taught to aspire to the position of national benefactors, teachers and helpers, and so to become exponents of the truest and wisest patriotism.

In the nurseries and schools of the world the principle of selfishness seems often to be exalted into a virtue. 'Preparation for life' seems all too often to consist in the cultivation of those aspects of the nature which have already done so much to create the misery which we see. The habit of self-interest, the 'duty' of competition, are taught from the earliest and most impressionable days by many who would be the last to work consciously and wilfully to impede the child's real growth. And children so taught, being left in ignorance of their own nature, its complexities and its intricacies, are unable to discriminate between the Higher Self and the lower, between the true and the false in life.

So-called spiritual education is too often confined to a single hour on one day in the week—a single hour once in seven days! Yet how few, even among the best and wisest, feel an obligation to train the spiritual Will and direct the abounding energies of their children—so tied down are they by false standards of home-life. Yet when these children grow to manhood or womanhood we are horrified to see, if not in their immediate family then in the community, the inebriate, the consumptive, the suicide, the criminal, the spiritual failure.

This is not a pleasant picture, but we should not shrink from it if we can learn a useful lesson and through the knowledge thus gained help the coming generations. I say this in no spirit of censure, believe me, for these mistakes are due in the main to the ignorance of the age, to false ideals in education, and to the lower psychology upon which we have been feeding the mind of man for centuries.

Music—and the Harmony Within

Music is one of the cornerstones of the Raja-Yoga system of education. The world has not yet awakened to its value as a factor in refining and purifying the character, especially during the early and more plastic years of life. It is a part of the daily life under the Raja Yoga system, not merely as an exercise which occupies its stated times and seasons, but as a principle which animates all the activities. The soul-power which is called forth by a harmony well delivered and well received does not die away with the conclusion of the piece. It has elicited a response from within the nature, the whole being has been keyed to a higher pitch of activity, and even the smallest of the daily duties, those which are usually called menial, will be performed in a different way.

The world has a wrong conception of the ideal in music, and not until it has rectified this can it perceive that true harmony can never proceed from one who has not that harmony within himself. What wonderful power lies in it to swing us out into the universal life. To realize its power is to realize that when self is forgotten, when personalities disappear, we are free—out in the open air of thought and love and the higher purposes. And yet even the best that we have today is but a materialistic expression in comparison with what it will be. Everything in music is so imperfect yet. We are but touching the fringe of the real harmony. If we could hold ourselves in the attitude of mind that is created when true music touches us; if we could bind and fasten ourselves to the larger views it opens out and broaden our comprehension of what life really means, we could tear down the veil that divides the seen from the unseen, the seeming from the real; we could look at life as it really is, at ourselves as we really are.

The Theosophist, who really desires to understand the soul of things, is ever careful in the selection of music, ever heedful as to what notes are sounded in the hearts of men, lest some great harm be done instead of good. There is an immense correspondence between music on the one hand, and thought and aspiration on the other, and only that deserves the name of music to which the noblest and purest aspirations are responsive.

There is a science of consciousness, and into that science music can enter more largely than is usually supposed. A knowledge of the laws of life can be neither profound nor wide which thus neglects one of the most effective of all forces.

Let us bring our children, therefore, close to the refining influences of the best in art and music. In doing so, however, let us realize that the power of beautiful expression in these things is not an affair of the intellect alone, nor of custom nor convention. Nor can it be learned from books. It comes from the awakening of the inner powers of the soul, those qualities of the nature which are in sympathy with whatever is high and pure.

Drama, Its Rightful Place

The drama, like music, is regarded by the world as one of the relaxations of life because it is supposed to deal with unrealities. True drama points away from unrealities to the real life of the soul. As such it should lead and guide the public taste, providing it with ideals towards which it can aspire. It is made to enter largely into the instruction of the students under the Raja-Yoga system, and nowhere are the advantages of this system more strikingly illustrated than in the dramatic power which can be called forth wherever there is an absence of self-consciousness and vanity.

Nowhere in the social life of today is the need for reform more manifest than in the drama. In too many directions it has been made to serve the sensationalism of the day and to stimulate the vicious thought which it might be so powerful to suppress. But we are within sight of the day which will restore the drama to its rightful position as one of the great redemptive forces of the age; for it is the heart that it reaches with its message. That is the secret of its power to regenerate.

Point Loma is a center from which streams of brotherly love radiate out into the world. The educational institution founded there has no other reason for its existence than to benefit humanity at large, to show that the life which is inspired by hope is necessarily the life which is rich in achievement, and that man does indeed possess to the fullest extent a dominion over Nature, vast and unimaginable. It has accomplished the mission which brought it into being. It has rescued Theosophy from the domain of an intellectualism which might easily have become more selfish, because more subtle, than the current thought of the world. It has demonstrated that the theosophic life is the life of practical common sense, and that in the light of its philosophy the shadows pass away and man can enter into his birthright of joy.

The inertia of custom and convention has been already broken, and the unrest of the world, at which so many look with distrust and apprehension, is but the movement of the ship with the incoming tide of purer and better thought. Ideals have been thrown out into the world, and because they are spiritual ideals they have entered into the minds of men and have painted entrancing pictures of what the world would be if man were but master of himself and of it. Those ideals will not die away until they have been realized, until they have given birth to other ideals which will illuminate forever the roadway of all future life, declaring the reality of a reign of peace on earth and of the god in man.

The Mystery-Drama

Men cannot be preached into compassion, nor sermonized into brotherly love, nor talked into love of justice. The virtues will not grow in the nature until the heart is touched, and the mystery-drama is the teacher's magic wand. For all dramas which give us a true picture of the soul's experiences and a true interpretation of the Higher Law and of life's diviner aspects are mystery-dramas, whether written by Aeschylus, or Shakespeare, or some unknown dramatist past or to come. Life is the great mystery, and in unveiling it, in the light of knowledge, the true drama has ever been and will ever be man's great instructor.

If one looks into ancient history, especially into that of Greece, one finds much that is both interesting and inspiring in connection with the religious aspect of the drama. There was a time when the Greeks, as many as thirty thousand of them, would meet in the morning and carry out their devotion to the superb religious dreams of their master-poets until sundown!

Thinking of this fact one can realize how much we have lost through the intervening years. It is only occasionally that one hears anything about the classical Greek dramas today. Of course, scholars are familiar with them to a degree; but the average person today, even among those who think, knows little about antiquity; and it is a great pity that the bread-and-butter question should be of such absorbing concern that much of the beauty and grandeur and inspiration and splendid spiritual support to be derived from the ancient dramas are lost.

One of the objects of the work which I represent is to create a greater love for the higher qualities of the drama, and to impress again upon the human mind through the drama the necessity for a religious view of life. To the ancients the drama was not merely a means of relaxation and amusement; it was a part of their religious life. And it is well known what lovers of the good, the true, and the beautiful the Greeks were.

There is a sanctification that comes from studying and working over one of these ancient dramas. I know that after each performance of *The Eumenides* here in our Greek Theater it takes me several days to come back to the everyday way of living.

Real drama affords man one of the grandest opportunities to understand himself. I refer particularly to the ancient Greek dramas. Practically every line in *The Eumenides,* for instance, contains a profound truth of the ancient Mysteries. The more one reads the more one desires to know about it. The more he studies the more enlightened he becomes. Here he sees clearly that man, being dual in nature, possesses on the one hand the attributes of the spiritual soul and the possibilities of great perfection; while, on the other hand, he has much in his nature that, unless he conquers it, will destroy him.

We should look upon human life as a great drama, a great mystery-drama filled with limitless possibilities. The kingdom of heaven is within; and so is the kingdom of hell, which is the kingdom of ignorance, of dissatisfaction, of delusion, and of unhappiness. If we wish to help to purify the world, to purify our nation, our city, and to breathe the sweet air of a new life, we must first allow ourselves to dream of the possibility of it. We must dare to go towards it and become the masters and understanders of our own lives first of all. Then we shall have the key to understanding the real drama of life.

8

FORESHADOWINGS

FORESHADOWINGS

From editorials appearing in 1897 and 1898

Are there not, in our civilization today, signs that mark a unique barbarism among us, showing an immense danger of retrogression? Can we not see, in spite of all the good there is in the world, that the very blood of some of our brothers is teeming with a heartless cruelty, a subtle viciousness, and a monstrous selfishness and hypocrisy? Is not the world brimful of unrest, unhappiness, injustice and despair; and are we not on the very edge of a condition which, if not improved, must sweep away bright prospects of our present civilization?

Today, as a people, we are by our thoughts and actions affecting to no small degree the record of the next century. We are adding one more link to the chain of events on both the lower and the higher planes of evolution. It is high time that we eliminate from our minds unfaith and egotism, cynicism and selfishness, and prepare ourselves to be a part of the great movement of spiritual life which is now close at hand.

The world seems mad today, moving towards a point at the end of this cycle where only staunch, firm, tempered hearts can turn this tide in the affairs of men to a higher plane of action.

I am not a pessimist, for I realize that despite the crimes and the disappointments and despair from which the world suffers today, there is a great promise of better things ahead. A change is coming. We are reaching the tether end of things as they are, and in the course of time something will happen that will suddenly arouse humanity to a realization that the only safe thing to hold to will be the great and inspiring truths of the majestic theosophical philosophy which is your rightful heritage.

Viewing the present striking aspects, can we for one moment be satisfied to live contentedly and selfishly in the shadow of darkness and unrest? It is possible for anyone having one grain of human pity in the heart, or love of truth and justice, to do aught but work, work, all the time unflinchingly and unselfishly, for his brother man and all creatures—not apart from but among them, with a courage that obscures all thought of self?

We should regard present events as transitory, leading to a more permanent and higher development. Indeed, we should learn practical wisdom through these varied and trying experiences. We must stand face to face with facts in the life of the world.

We can find light shining in dark places if we do not externally hold to forms and appearances. If we can but exert ourselves to think above the atmosphere of doubt and despair, we can find peace even amid the whirl and restlessness of life.

Now is the time, for at the end of this century an opportunity is given to humanity that it has not had for thousands of years. The cycle has reached its point of swiftest momentum. An effort made today has greater effect than at any other point of the cycle. It is like the ninth wave on the seashore which the fisherman waits for, that he may bring his smack safely to land. Today, a small effort brings great results; today sudden progress can be made that could not be accomplished before in months or even years. Today is the great opportunity to enter the Path.

But this cannot be accomplished unless men realize the essential divinity of their own natures. True progress begins with this step alone. Too long has poor humanity been living on the outer edge of truth and light; to long has help been sought from without; too long has the inner divine nature been obscured and the shadows of external life mistaken for the reality.

Unconsciously we may be playing into the hands of the Brothers of the Shadow by a careless thought, a lightly spoken word. We may thus strengthen their destructive work until what was in us a thought, becomes a terrific force, gathering momentum as it goes, until finally it results in some national calamity.

We cannot be too careful, let it be reiterated. The destiny of the nation lies in the hands of the people. Today we stand on the verge of great changes. Let us realize, then, our individual responsibility; let us by steadfast integrity uphold the true principles of brotherhood; and let us hope with that grander hope of the soul, the energy of right action, that the day is not far distant when the great sweeping force of Love—of true brotherliness—shall encompass humanity, when the knowledge of right living shall be in the grasp of all, and shall be lived in the truest sense of the word, when children shall be conceived and educated in the atmosphere of purest thought and grander action. Then, and not till then shall humanity commence to build the solid foundation of a golden age and work in the kingdom of freedom.

America must rise to something more than commercial prosperity or intellectual advancement. I believe that this great country is the chosen spot for solving some of life's greatest problems. But we must become more united and recognize the fact that brotherhood is a fact in nature. We must live up to it in all the smallest duties and all the time.

And so I say to the young: study the Constitution of the United States; go back to the spirit that actuated the formation of that Constitution. When I read it I feel myself in touch with the splendid minds who drafted it. They were so united in purpose, so lifted out of their own personalities, so imbued with the need of some splendid, inspiring hope for future generations, that they were "gathered together" in the real sense, as when Christ said "For where two or three are gathered together in my name, there am I in the midst of them."

Rich as America is, progressive as it is in many ways, it has not yet touched the key to that remedial power that alone can lift the burdens from the people. Something more than material wealth is needed, something more than intellectual accumulation.

At the close of the year 1897, amidst the turmoil and unrest engendered by the titanic forces of good and evil contending for the mastery of the coming centuires, are heard the cheery, silvery notes of the Christmas bells and the loving voice of the Christos, bidding men cease their selfish strife and their mad race for power and gain, calling them to turn their faces to the Light and unite their hearts and voices in one great anthem of brotherly love, of peace and good-will to all creatures; and urging us with courage and patience to brace our inner natures against all that seeks to lead us from the true Path, that we may gain greater strength to do our whole duty to our fellow-men.

It is impossible to gage the significance of the present time or to realize what is in store for humanity during the next hundred years, merely from our own experience and from recorded history. For this is no ordinary time; it is not simply the culminating point of the past hundred years, but of thousands of years. The night of the centuries has passed, and with the new dawn comes the return of memories and powers and possibilities of an age long past.

The soul of man still cries out, the darkness is still so close about him that he knows not the dawn is so near. But those who have climbed to the hilltops have seen the glow in the eastern sky and the rays of golden light in the heavens; and with the suddenness of the break of day in the tropics, in the twinkling of an eye, the light will come, the scales fall from our eyes, and we shall see —not in the uncertain gloom of night, but in the glorious sunlight.

As the light of day scatters the shadows and the powers of darkness, so will the effulgence of the new cycle break through the dark places of ignorance, prejudice and unbrotherliness in the age now so swiftly passing. The great heroes of old will once more return to earth; the great musicians, painters, poets, wise statesmen, lovers of the race, will again take up their loving task, and the earth shall blossom as a garden. The ancient wisdom taught in the sacred mysteries will be revived; the earth, the air, the ether, all nature, will reveal their secrets to those who have prepared themselves through purification and by service to humanity.

Such is the outlook into the future. To measure it, go back to the glory of ancient Egypt and to the yet older civilization and vaster achievements of ancient America. Such a future awaits us and our children, and if we are faithful, shall be ours in the new time when, after a brief night of death, we return to take up our work again upon earth.

9

INVOCATION

INVOCATION

O ye men and women! Sons of the same Universal Mother as ourselves! Ye who were born as we were born, who must die as we must die, and whose souls like ours belong to the Eternal: I call upon you to arise from your dreamy state and to see within yourselves that a new and brighter day has dawned for the human race.

This need not remain the age of darkness, nor need you wait until another age arrives before you can work at your best. It is only an age of darkness for those who cannot see the Light, for the Light itself has never faded and never will. It is yours if you will turn to it, live in it; yours today, this hour even, if you will hear what is said with ears that understand.

Arise then, fear nothing, and taking that which is your own and all men's abide with it in peace for evermore!

Out of the great heart of Nature all things proceed, and all things lead back there at last; all worlds and systems of worlds, from the great central sun to the smallest particle in space, must thrill responsive to the pulsations of that infinite heart of compassion. The great mother reaches forth to receive her own. All efforts to retard are less than insignificant. In every act which partakes of the divine quality of infinite compassion lies concealed the potency of all the spheres. All nature obeys the command of one whose heart beats constantly for others.

Oh that every atom in my being were a thousand-pointed star to help men see the divine everywhere, to know their limitless power, to feel while in the body the exhaustless joy of real life, to wake and live instead of dreaming the heavy dreams of this living death, to know themselves as at once part of and directors of Universal Law! This is your birthright of wisdom, and the hour of attainment is *now* if you will.

Tarry no longer in the delusion of the 'Hall of Learning'. Feel, Know, and Do! You are face to face with the defeats of the past, but in your hands is a new weapon forged in all past struggles. Wherefore arise, claim your own, move on to the sublime peace that shall follow the final victory!

Every time the wind blows it is singing you a song of the gods. Every time a flower blossoms it is bringing you a message from the Higher Law. Every time you hear the ocean as it beats against the shore and recedes in musical rhythm, it is speaking to your soul—a voice from nature, verily a voice from God. The magnitude, the grandeur of these things, the possibilities folded within them—these can truly be sensed only in the silence.

Every day has its brightness, its bloom, its color. Every day is the happiest I ever lived. There is no thought of yesterday or tomorrow, only the joy of living today, the happiness of the passing moment, the unity of all life and the noble plan of life universal. I see on one side forces of darkness, on the other those of Light; but I do not dwell on the dark side. I turn my eyes to greet the rising sun.

A new hope is dawning for humanity. This hope is the mainspring of progression and the evidence of it can be seen everywhere. The great heart of nature pulsates with joy, as it did in the days preceding the dawn of the dark age. Men and women who have so long borne the heavy burden of life, whose hearts have been well-nigh broken by the weight of many sorrows, feel the new joy awakened by the great symphonies of harmony which are now being sounded. It is felt in the heart of man and gives rise to constant aspiration. It is the quality which makes him great.

The golden light is shining. The herald of the morning proclaims the message of love anew. The ripples of the waves on the sea-shore lisp the glad song; the breeze bears it on its bosom; the tints of the flowers convey it; it shines forth from the stars in their sparkling brilliance; the great blue dome above suggests it; the birds warble it forth from every tree; the new-born babe is a complete revelation of it; the eyes of the loved ones passing into the great beyond impart the strength and courage of that great hope, and point to a future day when they shall return again to carry on their work. For hope incarnates from age to age, and where hope dwells, beauty and love abide forever.

The Law is immutable and Love is eternal.

As in every advance that nature makes—as the cycles in their wheeling course come round—there are some who lag behind and lose sight of their heritage blinded by the desire of personal gain, by ambition and love of power, so today there are some who refuse the opportunity that for ages their souls have waited for. The cycles have brought them and ourselves to the point of former achievement and former failure. We and they have met in the past as in this life, and shall meet again in the future, and by our action today we are forging the links that shall help or mar their progress, as well as our own and that of all humanity, in the future.

But the crucial point of the cycle is past; the fiercest ordeal is over. No powers in heaven or hell can longer stay the onward progress of humanity. The hosts of Light are already victorious. The anthem of Truth, Light and Liberation, Brotherhood, Peace and Joy, is echoing in the hearts of men. Arise, greet the morn! Salute with us the rising sun!

Children of Light, let us go forth into the world and render noble service to all that live!

O my Divinity! thou dost blend with the earth and fashion for thyself Temples of mighty power.

O my Divinity! thou livest in the heart-life of all things and dost radiate a golden Light that shineth forever and doth illumine even the darkest corners of the earth.

O my Divinity! blend thou with me that from the corruptible I may become Incorruptible; that from imperfection I may become Perfection; that from darkness I may go forth in Light.

APPENDIXES

APPENDIX I

THEOSOPHY AND SOME OF THE VITAL PROBLEMS OF THE DAY

[Under this title in January, February and March 1915 Katherine Tingley gave a series of extemporaneous lectures at the Isis Theater, San Diego, California. The following is the first address, given on January 10th. From it the reader may judge the substance and quality of her talks, and gather something of the inner drive to share the theosophical philosophy and way of life with her audiences characteristic of her hundreds of public addresses.]

H. P. Blavatsky and the Founding of the Theosophical Society

Owing to the fact that San Diego is crowded with visitors to the California-Panama Exposition, it is to be presumed that there are many strangers here tonight; and it is quite natural that there should be some who are unfamiliar with the history and work of the Theosophical Society, founded in New York City in 1875 by Mme. H. P. Blavatsky.

It has therefore occurred to me that it would be well to give you a short account of the foundation of the Society and its foundress. It was about forty years ago that Mme. Helena Petrovna Blavatsky left her native land, Russia, and a home of ease and comfort, surrounded by everything that would make life agreeable to the ordinary pleasure-seeker, and came to the Western World with a mission. On her father's side, she was the granddaughter of General Alexis Hahn von Rottenstern-Hahn (the representative of a noble family of Mecklenburg, Germany, settled in Russia); on her mother's side, the granddaughter of Privy-Councillor Andrew Fadeyev and of the Princess Helena Dolgorukov.

During the interval that elapsed between the time of her leaving Russia and of her coming to this country, she became intensely interested in the welfare of humanity, for she had marked the striking contrasts in human life, the great divisions in the human family—she found that brother was pitted against brother, nation against nation. She became convinced that the dogmatism and materialism of the age were growing, and that men were moving away from their best opportunities in life.

You should read our Theosophical literature, if you wish to become acquainted with her life-work and with the philosophy she taught, which she called the "Wisdom-Religion," because it is both scientific religion and a religious science. The teachings of Theosophy are fully set forth in her wonderful book, *The Secret Doctrine*, and in her other writings.

Reincarnation

Reincarnation was one of the most important doctrines introduced in her Theosophical teachings. It was only about forty years ago, that, to mention the word "Reincarnation," or to attempt to analyse this doctrine before an American audience was almost enough to insure the speaker being hissed from the platform. But the American people have made rapid strides in some ways; and we as a people are now accepting propositions which heretofore our prejudices and misconceptions would not permit us to consider. Today we are outgrowing some of our old ways, so that now we are setting aside the images that we had fashioned through our misconceptions and prejudices; new ideas are taking root in our minds, and are bringing us to a point of understanding, where we shall be able to take up all serious subjects from different viewpoints and handle them with that intelligence and devotion which all serious subjects demand.

I say let those who are interested in the advancement of the human race study the subject of reincarnation. One of the greatest possible proofs that I can bring to sustain my argument in favor of reincarnation is Mme. Blavatsky's own life and the work that she accomplished. This is the question which I have presented to some of the savants and brightest minds of the age, and also to some of the severest critics: Will you please explain how it was that Mme. Blavatsky acquired the knowledge which she has presented to the world in her writings? How could a woman of her apparently limited experience and of her youthful age, when she started her work, have gained in one life the comprehensive *insight* and the knowledge which she presents in her wonderful writings? Surely there is no other way to explain it, except to admit that she must have lived before, and that in her former lives, she had, through experience and study and investigation, garnered these glorious truths of Theosophy and held them to be used when the opportunity should present itself to her. That she was a woman of rare attainments and wonderful capabilities, intellectual and otherwise, cannot be questioned.

H. P. Blavatsky's Mission

There must have been a great urge in her life for her to have thought herself away even from her home environments, away from her worldly interests, away from her country to other countries and to other people. Realizing the needs of the great human family, her heart was moved; and she courageously stepped forth into a field of service. It was a colossal undertaking which she began. It was a tremendously great and serious work, and a perplexing one; but with the conviction that she had the needed knowledge, and with her love of humanity, there was a courage born of her urge which brought her to the Western World, where she introduced the teachings of Theosophy and organized the Theosophical Society in 1875. Although an able scholar in other languages, at that time Mme. Blavatsky was unfamiliar with English. This was a great obstacle in her way, which in the course of time she overcame. She began her work in New York City, and almost immediately attracted the attention of some of the most intellectual and progressive minds of the age—by whom she was considered a strange study.

In her efforts to teach and help she was ready to investigate all subjects; she pointed out with abundant logic the necessity of the ideas of Theosophy being implanted in the minds of the people of the present age; that these ideas might lead the people from dogmatism and materialism into a larger and broader life. She declared that unless humanity awakened to its real needs and to its opportunities, the human family as a whole must retrograde into the shadow and lose sight of the spiritual life and light that rightfully belong to every man.

Some of the Teachings of Theosophy

So it was that she establishd the Theosophical Society on entirely unsectarian and non-political lines. She accentuated tirelessly the truths of Theosophy; she declared that man's essential divine nature was a potent quality which should be aroused continuously: i.e., that man was dual in his nature—that the higher, the nobler, the divine part, was the corrective and inspiring part, and that the human mind, no matter how splendidly trained, must be controlled by this higher self: before this, man could not find his true place or realize his latent possibilities. She declared in her teachings that one who would know his strength, must find his divinity, not *outside* himself, but *within;* that he must understand the laws of evolution and involution; that spiritually he must realize that he is a part inseparable of the great human family; and that if he carried the investigation of Theosophy far enough, he would readily conceive of Deity as an all-powerful, omnipresent principle, rather than as a personal God existing at some point in space.

Theosophy, in its teachings of a Supreme Power, places Deity in quite a different light from that of the theologians; and let me assure you that it required courage on the part of Mme. Blavatsky publicly to declare these bold and daring ideas forty years ago. She accentuated the splendid optimism of Theosophy, whose illuminating teachings eliminate fear. She reminded all men that according to the teachings of Theosophy, no man is an "original sinner," in the theological sense; and that man must not depend upon certain redemptive powers *outside of his own divine nature* for salvation.

Theosophy soon began to take root in the minds of some of the most progressive characters in America and Europe; but Mme. Blavatsky continued her arduous work for many years, until now the teachings of Theosophy have spread throughout the world and have attracted to the membership of the Theosophical Society, not only the learned and the prosperous, but hundreds and hundreds of people who would otherwise be on the negative side of life, hopeless and despairing; for Theosophy gives encouragement and hope, and it shows that man's possibilities are greater than we dream, but that humanity is asleep and needs to be aroused, to be awakened to realize its latent power. When this is done, man will take up his life more understandingly; and as his mind opens to the light, he will realize the sacredness of his responsibilities, he will have more trust in himself, and more trust in his fellows. His conceptions of life—of the Essence of Life and of those higher laws governing man—will be so illuminating that a new courage will be born in him, and he will meet his sacred responsibilities with growing knowledge and real devotion.

Theosophy teaches that there is no such thing as chance in life, but that our lives are governed by immutable laws; and that as we work in consonance with these, on lines of least resistance, the mysteries of our own natures are more fully revealed to us. Then follows the strength for overcoming and for becoming. This brings us to a broader conception of human life, and to a wider sympathy, so that we shall be better able to enter into the fields of investigation and human effort for the upliftment of our kind.

Theosophy Not Opposed to Pure Christianity

Mark the contrast between these simple teachings and the old theological ideas which have been for ages obscuring the glorious and royal truths which belong to the nature, origin, and destiny of man. But pray bear in mind that Theosophy is not opposed to Christianity, pure and simple, as the Nazarene taught it; but it is opposed to all error; and consequently is opposed to "churchianity,"—to all forms, creeds, and dogmas, which blind the minds of men, and lead them from the true knowledge. To these things it is decidedly opposed; but in no sense is it opposed to the ideals of true Christianity.

It can readily be imagined that forty years ago, one declaring these unsectarian ideas and making an earnest effort to live up to them, and to establish a Theosophical Society, which would become a vehicle, in a way, of them, must necessarily have suffered some persecution; and Mme. Blavatsky did suffer persecution, and so did those who supported her and co-operated with her. And this persecution came mostly from a class of people who professed to be followers of the lowly Nazarene, of him who said: "Love ye one another." I would not have you think that I include in this statement all professed Christians—not by any means—but only a certain class. They still live, and are sometimes our neighbors. They are still so much attached to their creeds and their prejudices, to their dogmatism and their blindness, that they have failed to realize their responsibilities, and to recognize the glorious truths of the divine possibilities in man and the divine laws governing life and man. Such as these are held down by man-made dogmas, and are selfishly indifferent to the highest interests of humanity.

But I am sure that there are thousands and thousands of splendid, noble-hearted people upholding these dogmas and creeds in all sincerity—in a certain quality of faith; but surely not in knowledge; because if they had the real knowledge, if their faith were bringing them the spiritual strength that their hearts crave and their souls aspire to, death would be deprived of all its terror, for fear should have no place in a true Christian life. Theosophy teaches that if the spiritual light is shining, if the knowledge is in the life, fear disappears; and death, that awesome subject to most people, is robbed of its terror and its shadows and sorrow, and it stands out in quite a new meaning. Theosophy teaches that death is but rebirth; that man passes through different schools of experience in different lives, in order to evolve and ultimately to attain a state of perfection; and that when the body, which Theosophy teaches is the living temple of the Christos Spirit, is worn out, the soul is freed, not by death, but by a new birth, and moves on to other states, where it rests and gains strength to return to the earth-plane and take up its life on earth where it left it off. Only a few years ago the subject of Reincarnation was an unpleasant one to people of limited views and of not over-courageous natures; but now the wide-spread influence of Theosophy has brought about a revolution of thought and feeling on this subject; and there are thousands of people today who believe in it and depend upon it, as a great factor in adjusting their lives.

Reincarnation versus Heaven and Hell

The doctrine of Reincarnation affords great hope, great encouragement, and more spiritual light and incentive than one can possibly find in the old doctrines of a future state. The old idea that man is allotted but seventy-seven or a hundred years in this life, and then goes to a state of glory or to another place, is disappearing. According to the old theology, you know, there are but two alternatives, and there is no other choice. While we know that but few intelligent people accept the old doctrine today, there are still many who are preaching it—not with the intensity of forty years ago, but it is taught, it is suggested, and it is brought out in many ways directly and indirectly, and man is still reminded that a day is coming, when, unless he repents and accepts the means of salvation which are generally presented, he is lost.

Contrast this man-made system with the glorious, old teaching of Reincarnation, and tell me: Is not this doctrine worth investigating? Is it not a subject that one should try to understand? What a lift, mentally and spiritually, all humanity could receive through studying such a subject! Think of the optimism of it, the beauty of it, the inspiration of it, and the blessing of it! Yes, truly, the doctrine of Reincarnation means much to humanity; and I know that as the years go on and Theosophy becomes more wide-spread, the old ideas will die a natural death, the old theological teachings will disappear, and that those who now depend for salvation upon their creeds and dogmas, will modify their beliefs and ultimately have the courage to stand out as champions of the broader views of the great laws of life.

A Crisis in the History of Humanity

This is a pivotal time in the history of humanity, and we are having opportunities now that may never come again in this life—possibly never at all. Does not this awful war in Europe, which is reaching the very threshold of our hearts and of our national life, afford us a lesson which challenges us to higher and nobler efforts for the upliftment of humanity? Have we done our duty in the past to our fellows? Have we not, by our doubts, our half-heartedness, and our selfishness, assisted in the disintegration of those moral and spiritual forces which should hold all men at peace with one another and all nations in unity?

Your aim henceforth should be to try to refashion human life—first in the self, then by the example of courage, compassion, and knowledge, to impart strength to the faltering, the weak, and the discouraged. Oh, help, I pray, to break the bondage of the old ideas about man and his destiny! Clear the way for the coming generation, that it may find the light and live on a higher plane than we know of now! Through new endeavor and greater trust in the higher law, help to lift the burdens from the people, and make knowledge a potent factor in human life, instead of mere faith!

The children of this age are making a demand upon all humanity, upon our institutions, and upon the national and international spirit of our time. Depend upon it, our children are feeling this undercurrent—this new touch of liberation that is in the soul of thing; and they are pulling away from the old ideas which you were taught to bow down to and follow; and unless you substitute something practical, pure, and uplifting—unless you bring into their lives a new hope and more optimistic pictures for the future—you will fail in your duty to the children, and you will make for yourselves, by your acts of ommission, a karma which I feel sure you would not care to meet.

Men have been for ages drifting apart and are pathetically separated. It is because of this that they have lost sight of their larger responsibilities. Then too, the people of this age, in their limited view of human life, and in their uncertainty about the future, are growing careless in building their own characters and in so preserving their own bodies, that they may live out their fullest time and thus fulfill the law.

The Fear of Death

Fear is an ever-haunting power which stands as a phantom, overshadowing the best possibilities of man. The fear of death, shown in the preparations for its coming, in the material sense, and the letting go of the love of the nobler life, have not only stultified man's possibilities, but have deprived him of the joy that would be his, if he were on the real path of advancement. The fear of death! How it haunts poor humanity, and what cowards it makes of many!

In studying the history of the nations and of men, note how some of the greatest minds are shut off in this life, just when they begin to show signs of broadening their views and extending their service for the betterment of all. False teachings have left their mark even on the strongest minds and the strongest characters; and not until they are eliminated can man stand like a warrior and meet the vicissitudes of life with strength and courage and hope; not until he realizes his nearness to the Infinite, can he see beyond the grave, and dare to live in strength and purity on and on—even to a hundred years, with his faculties alive and his energies at his command until the last.

Let man no longer follow the lines of negation, but stand firmly for the positive forces in life. Let him win for himself, through self-conquest, the power to control his body and stimulate his mind to a broader view of human needs. We need new human laws of the kind that will breathe justice in every word, the kind that will touch the hearts of humanity and evoke a new co-operation. It is the song of brotherhood, of peace and good will to men, that must be the outgrowth of the heart-life of the world, which waiting humanity is calling for. Let humanity find a key to the true situation, before it is too late, and consider the first fifty years of life as years of serious preparation on the path of perfectibility, and the remaining years as but a higher school of thought and service. It is the afterglow of human effort that affords inspiration. Man's nature, mellowed and strengthened through suffering and experience, could stand out like a god, if man would but permit it, at the end of one mortal life, facing the next with a courage known only to the warrior.

Theosophy the Beacon-light

Ah, Theosophy! Theosophy! It is the great beacon-light! It stands in its colossal strength and its wonderful potentialities, as the Good Angel of the Twentieth Century. Let all turn to its teachings, and find the Lost Word, and through this, let each and all become imbued with the real spirit of brotherhood. Remember that we—the least of us—are all a part of the good universal life, and we are all enfolded in the compassionate divine law which governs all humanity; that within us is the Christos Spirit; that there is a living, spiritual power in our natures, ever seeking for higher expression. There is the "Knower"—the higher Ego, the Higher Self. It is something that can think above your brain-mind thinking, and dream dreams of life's possibilities, beyond all the dreams of the brain-mind. It is something that can fashion your mentality to the will of the Higher Law, and to the beauty and grandeur of spiritual life. If you will listen to its voice and its urge, it will eliminate from your mind doubts, fears, and heartaches, and tears; and it will crowd out the nightmares and delusions from your life, and fill your intellect with ideas, which, in the course of time, will lead you to real knowledge.

Real Peace: Universal Peace

I have dreamed of the time, possibly fifty years hence, when through the teachings of Theosophy, it will be almost impossible to see in the faces of humankind such suffering and despair. I have even dared to dream that under the beneficent power of these teachings, the peculiar unrest which fills all human life today will have died a natural death; that doubt, uncertainty, and selfishness will be shadows of the past. The many vital problems in human life which we have before us in our daily experiences, and through our general observation, challenge us for nobler effort; and many lose hope of any change. Not having faith in themselves, they have no faith in the future. I admit that it is difficult for us to see how we are to meet all the pressures which are upon us, with any degree of knowledge which will prove beneficial —particularly at this time of international unrest when it seems as though one half of the human family were struggling to destroy the other half; when the very air is pregnant with the insanity of the age—unbrotherliness.

I am not ready to say that peace—permanent peace—can be established through even the best efforts of our greatest statesmen and most sympathetic people. If we are to have permanent peace and are to hope for a permanent unity among the nations and peoples, we must necessarily follow a new line of thought and action, and there must be hearty and splendid co-operation manifest before the subject could be successfully approached. We would have to start out with the idea that we were building for eternity; and the seeds that we sow today must bring a rich harvest in the life of the coming generation. We would be obliged to carry in our lives that sweet touch of practical human brotherhood, which would give us the inspiration to meet all these issues and to call upon the people for the establishment of a new order of ages.

Humanity has been startled by the pictures of suffering and sorrow and death. Why not awaken it under the beneficent influence of promised joy? Let us accentuate the spirit of brotherhood in our natures—of unselfish, noble brotherhood. Demand it of the people and of the nations. Work for the spiritual regeneration of man, free from creeds and dogmas. Work and work! This would be prayer of a potent quality!

Do you believe for a moment that the brightest minds of the age—representatives of the different nations, our greatest statesmen—could meet today and fashion any possible scheme by which we could have continued peace? We all know it would be but temporary; that if treaties were made they could be broken, as treaties have been made and broken. We know that in spite of the best efforts that could be presented, wars must come in the course of time, and more suffering and despair, ignorance, and crime.

So, with this picture of humanity as it is, and our national and international life as it is, can we not build for the more beautiful picture—that optimistic and inspiring one which must shed a light over all humanity, because of its spiritual growth?

Theosophy in the Home

Here is another problem: the home-life. Are the mothers and fathers and the educators and the progressive minds of the age satisfied with the home-life of the

Twentieth Century? Are *we* satisfied—knowing as we do, what the hime-life is among the majority of the people of today? Do we not all realize that under the present régime the future generation can have but little of the greater hope? Are not crimes increasing—crimes unspeakable? Are we not reading from day to day, in our daily newspapers, the stories of youthful crimes? Are we not meeting the harvest of our acts of omission in the past, and our failure to make home-life what it should be?

The question naturally arises: What can bring a change for the better in the home-life? What factors can be introduced to readjust it and bring it nearer to perfection? Theosophy answers that the parents should begin to study the higher laws of life and the great responsibilities of fatherhood and motherhood even before marriage. Home should be acclaimed as the center from which the higher life for the nations should spring.

Theosophy says: Build spiritual altars in the home. Let the parents spend as much time in accentuating the spiritual laws of life in the family, as they do in caring for their worldly needs and pleasures, and the impermanent things of life. How inspiring is the picture of a home that has been really touched by the teachings of Theosophy! I open the door on such a one, and before me I see the little children gathered about the home-altar, grasping even in their childhood life, some of the teachings which are necessary to help them to build and fashion their own characters. They are being taught the divine laws governing us all, and not the least is overlooked. Even little children can assume responsibilities, which can be brought out through the co-operation of the parents. But the parents must not only understand, they must have learned to live the life, and be sincere and inspiring examples of real parenthood. I linger on the threshold of such a home, and feel in its atmosphere that the Kingdom of Heaven on Earth has already begun.

Let the coming generations see the preciousness of

human life, and the splendor and royalty of it. Permit the children to be imbued with a love for the higher harmonies, and a distaste for anything that would mar the charm of home. Oh, what power and what enlightenment would then creep into the lives of the parents! Make the home the center of the true and ennobling life. Make it beautiful and attractive, even though it be simple. Cultivate music and the love of art and literature in the home. Make these an active part of the home-life. Parents living in such an atmosphere as I have depicted, would guard the sacredness of home in a new way, and would realize more fully the sacred ties of marriage and the responsibilities belonging thereto.

As I have often said before, when woman finds her true place in life, man will find his. When woman realizes the true power of motherhood and its responsibilities, then man will also awaken to his duties in this connexion. Then we can conceive that home-life built on a solid foundation of spiritual life, will bring a higher and richer expression of joy than we have ever dreamed of; and that true marriage would be an eternal courtship. My listeners may think this is a far-fetched dream which I have presented; but you see, I have more faith in humankind and its possibilities than those have who might criticise me or my word-pictures. I marvel that the men and women of the age do as well as they do, when I consider what they have been deprived of—deprived of the opportunity to understand the true science of life.

The bread-and-butter question is a hard one, and many a brave man and woman have sunk under the pressure of it. But let the men and women, the builders of the home, find their strength through the teachings of Theosophy. This will give them the knowledge and the courage to overcome obstacles and to win for all time; for those who have failed, have not had the knowledge. Consequently they have not had the courage. Not having faith in themselves, they have lost faith in their fellows and in their future; but a new trust can be born—an inspiring courage can come, when man has found his essential divinity—the key to all the problems of life; when man has found the sweetness and the glory of spiritual life, and has so fashioned himself that the whole life is one practical, helpful expression of all that is noblest and best.

[Another address in this series was given on February 21, 1915, preceded by eight short talks by representatives of the Men's Theosophical League of Humanity. The San Diego *Union* of the following day reported this meeting as follows, under the heading of "Theosophy's Aims Elucidated by Speakers—Mme. Tingley and Others Explain Objects of World-Wide Movement":]

The meeting last night at Isis was of unusual interest for the reason that it gave the large audience present an opportunity of learning something of the Men's Theosophical League of Humanity, of its aims and the ideals which actuate its members. As was explained by one of the speakers, its objects are in the main similar to those of the Women's International Theosophical League. It was further explained that Mme. Tingley's object in organizing these two leagues was to bring about the perfect cooperation of men and women along all lines, and particularly those of practical humanitarian work.

Stage Attractively Decorated

The stage setting was effective. In front and on the wings were the usual beautiful decorations of foliage and flowers. In the center of the stage was an altar of white roses, back of which were seated some twenty members of the Men's League. Behind these, on a raised platform, was the Râja-Yoga International Orchestra of some forty-five performers, which during the evening rendered the following selections. Overture, *Egmont*, (Beethoven); *To a Water-Lily*, (MacDowell); Barcarolle from *Tribute of Zamora* (Gounod); March from *Aïda* (Verdi). During intermission one of the students of the Isis Conservatory of Music sang a tenor solor, *Homeward* (Franz Abt).

Brotherhood Essential

The meeting was opened by Clark Thurston, president of the League, who welcomed the audience as guests of Mme. Tingley and of the members. He explained that the purpose of the League was the practical application of Theosophy and Brotherhood to the needs of humanity. The atmosphere of Brotherhood, he said, was alone that in which the spiritual life could find expression. The truths of Theosophy during the forty years since they were again presented to the world by Mme. Blavatsky, the foundress of the present Theosophical Movement, have, to a great degree, changed the currents of human thought, he said.

J. H. Fussell, secretary of the Universal Brotherhood and Theosophical Society and private secretary to Mme. Tingley, spoke of the purpose of both the Men's and Women's Leagues, which, he said, was to help humanity. "This purpose," he said, "is two-fold. On the one hand it is to lessen the world's suffering, its sorrow and its heart-ache, by removing all those obstacles which impede human progress, all forms of unbrotherliness, cruelty and injustice; and on the other it is to inculcate those high ideals of conduct which are the opposite of these and upon the practice of which depend the future happiness and welfare of the world."

Soul must be Identified

Prof. F. S. Darrow, A. M., PH. D. (Harvard), declared man's mission to be to study his own dual nature, to learn to guide the outer material nature by the god within. "True happiness," he said, "can come only through unselfish striving; the path of progress knows no end; the soul as the child of the infinite must itself be infinite."

According to R. Machell, Director of the Art Department of the Râja-Yoga College, every man has to meet the question, "What is man's mission?" and he answers it by his life. "Man has ever two opposing ideals before him," said Machell, "that of giving and that of getting; altruism and egotism. Between these two man must and does choose, whether he will or no, and his life shows his choice."

J. F. Knoche, local business manager of the International Theosophical Headquarters, discussed the reasons why the study of Theosophy is of vital importance to the business man of today. "A fuller understanding of man's nature and possibilities is needed," he declared, "if man would not be a failure." This understanding, said the speaker, may be gained from the study of Theosophy.

Prof. W. A. Dunn, director of the Isis Conservatory of Music, spoke of the incongruity of man's accepting the reign of law over external nature without acknowledging its equal reign over man's moral nature. "Man's mission," he said, "is to co-operate with the laws of his moral and mental being equally as with the laws of his physical being. A strong and pure character can come only from perfect obedience to the laws of the spiritual life."

Disillusions of Life

Iverson L. Harris, Professor of Law of the Râja-Yoga College, spoke of the disillusions of life and of the mistakes people were liable to make who considered themselves disillusioned. He claimed that Theosophy had a message for such people in particular.

"Man's mission is to be God's warrior," said Kenneth Morris, a member of the Theosophical Headquarters literary staff. "We must fight or die; between morning or night one wins or loses as many battles as there are moments. It is the concern of all men to make the moments of the day divine. Man is a fighting animal when he is not a fighting god."

After a brief selection by the Râja-Yoga International Orchestra, Mme. Tingley appeared on stage. . . .

ADDRESS BY KATHERINE TINGLEY

Friends: I greatly appreciate the close attention you have given to the program which has been presented to you tonight, and if it were my choice I should prefer that the meeting closed at this moment; but since I am named on the program to speak, I am expected to do my part. As the time is limited, I shall say but a few words; that is, I would impress you with the importance of the study of Theosophy,—with the knowledge of these sublime truths that every human being should make a part of his life. These teachings are truly magnificent truths and they bring home to every man a hope and a consolation that no other teachings do, for the reason that they are based, not only on the soundest principles, but on knowledge. If one has true knowledge, and applies it to his life, he cannot fail to find happiness.

It may interest you to know that the gentlemen here tonight, who represent the Men's International Theosophical League of Humanity, are from different parts of the world—from England, Ireland, Germany, France, Holland, Sweden, Denmark, Australia, Canada, as well as from the United States; they are living at the World's Theosophical Center at Point Loma, and are endeavoring to cultivate the spirit of true brotherhood. Among them are a number who were pupils of Madame Blavatsky in the early days of the Theosophical Work, and who have since that time continued with determined effort, under the leadership of William Q. Judge, and with me, to sustain the Cause they love so well—Theosophy.

While looking at this earnest body of men, I have been impressed with the far-sightedness of Madame Blavatsky, for when she came to the Western World to re-introduce the unsectarian teachings of the Wisdom-Religion and to organize the Theosophical Society, she must have realized more than any of us can know, not only the great needs of humanity, but also that there were hundreds and thousands of hungry hearts awaiting her coming, calling for that help that her message would bring. Indeed, she must have realized in the silence of her heart and soul, the World-need. Well she knew that there were waiting souls the world over seeking opportunity to find the Path, whereby they might find themselves and thus become higher expressions of manhood and womanhood, and better helpers of the human race.

Truly great was her prevision of the World-need and of the hope and help that Theosophy would bring to men; for all over the world today we have representatives, not only of the Universal Brotherhood and Theosophical Society, but of these two Theosophical Leagues, the Woman's League and the Men's League, working together.

Let me assure you that you have caught but a glimpse here tonight of what the workers in these Leagues are doing. Both the men and the women work together. They are not seeking self-aggrandizement, nor aiming to receive public recognition or honors. They are serving without any salary or expectancy of reward, except to feel that they are lifting as best they know how, some of the burdens of humanity, and that they are bringing home to the hearts and minds of people of all nations, consolation and encouragement.

I recall a verse written by an Oriental. The lines are appropriate and suggest much thought. The title is "Man and Woman."

Are we not the tunes of the same one dream?
Are we not the stars of the same one gleam?
Are we not the fruits of the same one tree?
Are we not the waves of the same one sea?

Here is the keynote. Men and women have come from the same source, are seeking the same goal, are a part of the great universal life, are guided by the universal laws of being—each one of the two in place: the woman in her place, the man in his; the outward aspects different, with duties different, but the heart-hunger the same, and the spiritual will the same.

Can you not see that men and women such as I speak of, united as co-workers for the common good of humanity, must be able in the quiet of self-forgetfulness and in aspiration and devotion, really to do something more than is being done elsewhere today? Are they not bringing home to the minds of men that brotherhood is in fact a reality in nature? Separateness exists only because the human race has not the understanding of the laws of being—it has lost its way.

So Madame Blavatsky, that whole-souled Russian woman, realizing that the way must again be shown to men, gathered the ancient teachings, the principles of the Wisdom-Religion, which precede Jesus' time and that of other teachers—garnered them, held them in her heart all through her life, infused them into her books and into all her acts, and brought them to the Western World, and laid them at the feet of humanity.

No wonder that hundreds and thousands of people all over the world sought this Teacher; no wonder also that she was persecuted and misunderstood! But this was only by a class of people who had not studied their own inner being and who knew little or nothing of this inner knowledge that Theosophy gives. Never having sounded the depths of their own consciousnesses, in their blindness and egotism, they were ready to destroy the torch-bearer, who came to the world to bring them the very light that they most needed.

Madame Blavatsky did not claim to have any special spiritual powers; she did not place herself before the world as a Savior; she asked for neither adoration nor laudation—no sacrifice for her! She did not proclaim that *she* was the light, but simply declared herself to be a friend of humanity, a woman with a mission, a messenger bringing the ancient truths of the Wisdom-Religion to the people of the nineteenth century; and all that she asked of her students was to study Theosophy and to apply it in all their daily duties, and thenceforth to begin to live in a new way, and to serve in a new way—according to the highest dictates of conscience.

People sometimes question members of our Society and myself, and ask, "Why such enthusiasm? What is this telling power behind you that keeps you so cheerful and optimistic, that sustains you in your service to humanity, without salary or expectancy of reward? What is the wonderful power that holds your Society together so harmoniously?—that is the greatest wonder of all! And furthermore, what is the force that keeps the representatives of the different countries—representatives even of the warring nations in your Society—working in such a friendly spirit?" I answer, "It is the inner knowledge that I have spoken of, acquired by the students. They are endeavoring to round out their characters and to enlighten their minds, and to build for the future; indeed, they have sounded, to a degree, the depths of their consciousness. And they realize also that while they should hold to the highest spirit of patriotism for their respective countries, yet the international spirit is higher, and that one's own country can be better served by cultivating a right royal soul-patriotism, divine patriotism, justice to all people and all countries; that the most unselfish purposes must mark the life of the followers of Theosophy for the benefit of the people of the whole world—our common home."

In meeting you tonight, and in having invited my comrades to be present and represent the Men's International Theosophical League of Humanity and the Universal Brotherhood and Theosophical Society, I feel a very rich reward, for I know that most of you have been intensely interested and appreciative. Here tonight are my comrades, men of culture, men who are devoting their lives to their own and their fellows' betterment; these are men of strong will, of intense determination; and I am satisfied that nothing can hold them back from following the path they have chosen. Yes, they are trying to live out the Theosophical life fearlessly; and in protesting against the errors of the age and the persecution that the Society they represent has met with, they hold compassion even for the enemies of our work. They realize that those who would obstruct the path of a reformer who knows what he is about, have not sounded the depths of their own consciousness, and that they have not had the fight that those whom they persecute have; that some time far back in some life or other, they have wandered away from the blessed knowledge of their divinity; and that they are truly lost in delusion. They have been building on faith, or perhaps on mere prejudice, while the Theosophist builds on knowledge, knowledge of himself and of nature, for this is what Theosophy gives.

It is my hope that the utterances of my comrades on the value of Theosophy have stimulated you to new action, or renewed actions, on many lines; have given you new hopes and added courage. Many more interesting facts could have been given to you by my fellow-workers, if their modesty had not held them from telling you of their experiences and victories. They would indeed have lifted the veil from the work of the two Leagues of this Society—the Woman's League and the Men's League—and they would have shown you what splendid results they are achieving for the world's good. In truth, their work is far-reaching; it touches all classes of people and many deplorable conditions in life, from the highest strata of society down to the unfortunates in prison and out of it, to the deluded, the discouraged, and the despairing.

What pathetic stories could be told of their experiences with their fellow-men! Indeed, it is my firm belief that in later years the record of the work that the members of the Universal Brotherhood and Theosophical Society have done and of what they will do, will be passed down to posterity as the bible of the twentieth century. And then in all the other departments of human activity—in the scientific, the literary, the educational, the philanthropic, in business, and in fact on all lines, you will find they are meeting the vital problems of the day most intelligently and helpfully.

My final words to you tonight will express the pleadings that I so often present to my hearers here—study our Theosophical literature. Become acquainted with those heroic workers for humanity, Madame Blavatsky and William Q. Judge, through their writings; for these contain information and suggestions that every human being should know. Let us remember the following words from the Bible, so applicable to all human needs, that we may find strength therefrom, and do our whole duty all the time, all along the way: "If any man do His will, he shall know the Doctrine."

APPENDIX II

LETTERS FROM EGYPT

[The theosophical world tour, or Crusade as it was called, conducted by Katherine Tingley is well described by Emmett A. Greenwalt in *California Utopia: Point Loma 1897-1942.* It began in New York City in June 1896 and culminated at Point Loma, California, in February 1897. Lively meetings had been held in England and Ireland, and the party had then traveled through France, Holland, Germany, Switzerland, Austria, Italy, Greece, and again held public meetings in India, Australia and New Zealand. It was in October of 1896 that they were in Egypt; and printed in the Society's official magazine *The New Century* (Vol. I, Nos. 5 through 11, October 28 to December 11, 1897) were a series of short articles by Katherine Tingley recounting incidents of this visit. Though not of marked historical import, and more in the nature of letters written home, they yet register something of the atmosphere of those days, and so are included in this volume.]

It was a bright morning in the early part of October, 1896, when a party of seven American travelers (the Crusaders) found themselves facing the land of Egypt, off Alexandria. The steamer had just anchored and all was confusion on board.

The sun shone in great brightness over the tops of the mosques and the palace of the Khedive; the water was smooth as glass, reflecting the rays of the sun, forming a splendid and picturesque scene. The half naked natives, in their peculiar and many-colored garments, with their dusky skins and bright faces, paddling along in their small boats towards the ship, presented a fascinating finish to the scene. With a rush and a howl they climbed on deck, approached the passengers and baggage, almost throwing them overboard in their attempt to capture them for freight. The clamor and clatter reminded one of the old historic days when Babel was being built and many tongues prevailed. It was a strange confusion of languages very seldom heard, presenting quite a different aspect from that usually obtained by reading the rather dull accounts of Egyptian life and scenery. Everything was inspiring and lively. At the time when Cook's agent loomed up, the natives moved off in silent respect and way was made for the Americans to disembark for Alexandria. This representative was a native of statuesque and dignified presence in the gorgeous Egyptian style, and he bowed us into the boat as if we represented the whole kingdom of America, with a peculiar grace which was really charming. In a few minutes we reached the landing and were soon at the station to take the cars for Cairo.

While we sat in the station panting for breath, for it was insufferably hot, we cooled our thirst and ate our fill from the baskets laden with many bounties which the eastern natives carry about on their heads. Their beseeching eyes seemed to be more eloquent than words appealing for a few American pennies to keep their half-starved bodies, for while these people represent nominally a great race, they are a forlorn and unhappy people with but little to make life worth living.

Our ride that day along the Nile will never be forgotten. On one side stretched for miles the railroad track; on the other side could be seen the camels moving majestically over the burning sands laden with their heavy burdens, led by the natives clad in their loose flowing dresses. Time has worked no change in the methods of traveling; it is the same now as it was thousands of years ago.

After several hours ride, with which each moment was occupied in seeing the different pictures that presented themselves, Cairo was reached. This great city is located on the eastern bank of the Nile and is the largest in Africa; it is said to have 500,000 inhabitants. Some say it was founded by the Babylonians 525 B.C. and others that it was built by Semiramis. The writer presumes to say that it was founded in the times of Rameses II, and was built upon the ruins of a great city dating far back into prehistoric times.

Cairo, the oriental city with all its varied and novel attractions, had no interest or charm for us that day. Our voyage across the Mediterranean Sea from Greece to Alexandria, and the long, hot journey over the dry sands of the desert, with the discomfort of a poorly ventilated railway carriage, had served to make us feel too fatigued to enjoy anything but a good bath and rest. I question if ancient Egypt in all her splendor had loomed up before us whether we could have been sufficiently interested to appreciate its grandeur.

The hotel was soon reached, baggage unloaded, and then, even before we had engaged our rooms, the mail from America was placed in our hands. Letters from America! (bless the hearts that wrote them) messengers from home! How they cheered us and helped us dispel that awful feeling of homesickness which even the stoutest heart sometimes experiences when separated from its native land.

A good night's sleep had the desired effect of resting and refreshing the whole party. We had renewed our courage and were ready for the day's trip. Our Arabian dragoman (guide) arranged all the details even to a bountiful lunch, which we were compelled to carry, for we should not return until night. Our conveyances were the ordinary victorias. We drove through the narrow winding streets (near many that were inaccessible except to pedestrians and donkeys) crowded with camels, donkey-men, water-carriers, natives with their baskets of fruit on their heads; passed low shops with their windows filled with gorgeous fabrics and Eastern merchandise; saw the gorgeous palace, imposing mosques, the minarets and the harems with their projecting balconies enclosed in close lattice work; gazed in admiration at the great moving throng of people—the picturesque oriental scene of the Arabs, Mussulmen, Bedouins, Greeks, Armenians and Jews in their national costumes mingling with the plain and circumscribed dressed Europeans and the English soldier in his uniform of red and gilt. The last two types looked stiff, *outré* and unpicturesque.

Our drive lay along the broad shaded carriage road from which could be seen a small fellah village (composed mostly of low-roofed mud huts), and the Nile flooding the banks of the green fertile fields. Soon our eyes rested upon the monster structures of the pyramids and Sphinx—imposing, inspiring and awesome, they stood out like great sentinels—the protectors and preservers of the hidden mysteries of hoary antiquity.

Under the shadows of the Great Pyramid the Crusaders stood in silence meditating . . . and there came to the mind of the writer the truly inspiring words of Napoleon: "Soldiers, remember that twenty centuries look down upon you." The profound stillness that filled the atmosphere was broken by the wild cry of the Bedouins, about thirty in number, who were guarding the palace. They rushed towards us, pushing their camels, bowing and moving about in a noisy way, howling backsheesh and in broken English urging us to ride on their camels. In spite of the clamor and confusion we had a feeling of kindness in our hearts for these people, a larger charity possibly than the ordinary tourist, for were they not our brothers? The isolation of their lives and their limited opportunities of gaining a livelihood made us forget our annoyance at the persistent way in which they tried to attract our attention.

While some of the Crusaders went into the King's chamber through a narrow passage which opened at the middle of the Pyramid and others climbed up the huge side of it, the Bedouins were invited, the dragoman acting as interpreter, to listen to the writer who explained the mission of the Crusade. By this means the spirit of real brotherliness was infused into their hearts, for they listened attentively, smiled, gesticulated to each other expressing delight, and quietly sat down on their camels. After the speaker had finished they expressed pleasure at receiving so much kindness from strangers and said we appeared to them as different from other Christians they had seen. Later, one of their number approached our party. He was the grand Sheik of the Pyramid whom all his followers looked up to with great respect. In spite of the instinctive disregard these people have for women the Sheik was most courteous. He offered himself as a special escort to the writer, leading the way to the Sphinx and temple. Fancy the picture! The dignified and gorgeously dressed Sheik arm in arm with a modern dressed American lady walking through the deep sands of the Egyptian desert, and the other Crusaders following behind, seated on the backs of the stately camels which were led by the Bedouins. In the conversation the Sheik became so absorbed in the description of America that he seemed entirely unaware of the picture he presented with the lady's umbrella held down over his own well browned face, while his companion was exposed to the broiling rays of the sun. It was an amusing picture truly, and one not easily forgotten.

The Great Pyramid which we had recently passed was built by Khufu (or Cheops) B.C. 3733. His name was discovered on the inside written in red upon the blocks of stone. The stone used in this magnificent structure was brought from Turra and Mokaltana, and the whole amounted to eighty-five million cubic feet; the height of the pyramid is 451 feet.

Herodotus gives the following account of the building of the pyramid:

"Now, they told me to the reign of Rhampsiurtus there was a perfect distribution of justice, and that all Egypt was in a high state of prosperity. For that having shut up all the temples he, Cheops, first of all forbade them to offer sacrifices, and afterwards he ordered all the Egyptians to work for him: some accordingly were appointed to draw stones from the quarries in the Arabian mountains down to the Nile: others he ordered to receive the stones when transported in vessels across the river; and to drag them to the mountains called the Libyan.

"And they worked to the number of one hundred thousand men at a time. The time during which the people were thus harrassed by toil lasted ten years on the road which they constructed; a work, in my opinion, not much less than the Pyramids, for its length is five stadias—3050 feet—and its width ten orgyae, or forty-eight feet, and it is of polished stone with figures carved on it. On this road ten years were expended in forming the subterranean apartments of the hill on which the Pyramids stand.

"Over twenty years were spent in erecting the Pyramid itself. It is composed of polished stone and jointed with great exactness. None of these stones are less than thirty feet. The Pyramid was built in the form of steps which some call crossae, other bomedes. When they first built it they raised the remaining stones by machine made of short pieces of wood. Having lifted them from the ground to the first range of steps, it was put on another machine that stood ready on the second range; and so on, for the machines were equal in number to the ranges of steps. The highest part was first finished, and afterwards they finished the part below, and last of all they finished the part on the ground."

A most interesting conversation was kept up with my Bedouin friend as we slowly trudged along through the deep sands. He had heard something about America. He supposed it was a small place and that Chicago was the larger—"a great Mecca." When I made an attempt to answer some of the questions he had asked me about the habits of the American people, he grew quite excited and said: "Yr, yr, layde, me see some day great free country; me know how be good some day; me me must backsheesh work do now."

Many curious things he told me of his people, their customs and beliefs, and one could readily discover that these crude, uneducated Bedouins recognize an esoteric side to their religion. With a shrug of his shoulders he said, looking very stern and wise: "Bad fools hide Mahomet. Mahomet's life tells better than book; America don't know."

How true, I thought, was the statement of this simple man; books often misled us, writings of the ancient sages such as Buddha, Zoroaster, Confucius and the great Nazarene, poorly convey to one's mind any real knowledge of the inner lives of these men. One has to read between the lines, look behind the form, the letter, of these writings to understand their deeper meaning and to get the touch of the great Heart Doctrine which they taught.

The next moment we came to a halt, for just beyond was the colossal figure of the Sphinx, standing out in bold relief, facing the east. The Egyptians call the Sphinx Hern-em-chut, or Horus, the Rising Sun. He was the conqueror of darkness, the god of the morning. The Sphinx is hewn out of solid rock, the body about one hundred and fifty feet long; the paws, fifty feet; the head, fifty feet. From the top of the head to the base of the monument the height is seventy feet. At one time it was covered with limestone, its head bright red, but there are no traces of anything of the kind now.

In front of the Sphinx there was found in 1816 three small hieroglyphical tablets arranged like a naos, dedicated by the monarchs Thothmes III and Rameses II to the Sphinx. No information concerning the proportions of the Great Sphinx can convey to the reader the thrilling impression which it creates. There it lies, reposing on the sands as one in eternal waiting. Thousands of years have passed since it was placed in its present position, the eternal emblem of mystic silence, from which proceeds that knowledge of self which unveils in secret to the soul the mysteries of life and death and the Cause of Being.

As my Bedouin friend and I stood speechless before it, gazing at those eyes which seemed to contain within themselves infinite depth of knowledge, those thin, passionless lips, eloquent in their silence, there seemed a spell in the atmosphere holding all who beheld that calm, majestic figure. The mystery of the place was so great that the need of words seemed something which belonged to a remote past. We understood each other without speech. This, thought I, is prophetic of the time when all mankind shall comprehend one another without that medium —when knowledge shall be the fruit of silence. I thought of our Western world, of the time when it should wake from its hurry and bustle, its never ending stream of words, words, words, which generate all forms of excitement, and should know the stillness and repose of mind and heart, from which alone comes the abiding knowledge of Self. As I stood there I seemed to hear a soundless voice, saying: *Behold! I was begotten in the Silence of the Mighty Past. Born in the mysteries, from them I came. I am the key. Oh man, in me is contained the secret of all Eternity! In me the unchanging symbols of all time. If thou wouldst know the mysteries of Soul, of life and death, thou must look within. Thou hast the key. Thou art the Eternal Sphinx!*

The Sphinx still held my attention while my heart pulsated to the vibration of those magic words, and as they seemed to die away in space there was a sense of a deeper silence, a more subtle touch, such as one may feel but once in a lifetime.

Surely, thought I, if the great throbbing mass of humanity could understand, if they could once grasp the real meaning of life, and perceive the eternal golden thread of divinity that binds all in all, then their souls would be unbarred, and no longer would they be content to live on a material plane of selfishness and error, for the white light of their souls once freed, would illumine the world, and the glory of a departed peace and a true spirituality would return again.

The intense heat of the scorching sun and the voices of my comrades caused me to awaken from my reverie, and with my companion I moved on over the shifting hills of sand to the temple where the rest of the party were dismounting from their camels.

We soon found a shady corner in one of the halls of the temple and gladly sat down to rest ourselves. Just outside the camels lay crouching in the sands, with the attendant close beside them standing in an expectant attitude, ready to spring into action at a moment's notice. The Sheik and two of his companions moved off a short distance and sat down in the shade of one of the lofty columns. Through the opening side of the temple the sun threw its soft golden light in upon the granite and alabaster walls. A few hundred yards away could be seen the stately Sphinx and majestic Pyramid, the river Nile, and the wide stretch of green fields forming a striking and magnificent picture.

We were all affected by the solemnity and beauty of the scene as we sat gazing in wonderment and silence.

Even the group of the three who sat near seemed to take part in our thought and to enter into the spirit of the occasion with us.

There was one among them whom I had first noticed at the Pyramid; he was strangely unlike the rest of his companions, even in his dress, though his skin was dark and he was a Bedouin. His face was interestingly handsome and its expression peculiarly subtle and spiritual. He did not make the slightest effort to intrude himself or seek to impress us with his importance by assuming a mysterious air as is often done by those who pretend to possess some special inner knowledge. It was plainly seen that he was vastly superior in intellectual and spiritual attainments, and I was not surprised to find that he spoke English fairly well and knew a great deal about subjects such as interest only the thinking and scientific mind.

When I asked him where it was that he had gained his knowledge, his face lit up with a curious and knowing smile, and he said, "I go away some time to my Teacher and I come back again when my people need me."

"Luncee for the Kusady," called out our Arabian attendant, the dragoman, as he flourished about with the air of a prince, and he looked it every inch too—he was almost a perfect type of a young oriental in his gorgeous and rich dress of pale yellow and purple silk and red velvet fez.

Without formality we sat down to our lunch spread on the rock floor of the temple with no end of tempting things before us, and ate heartily, for we were very, very hungry, filling in the time between courses with talks of home and Crusade experience. One of our members, the jolliest of all, with a sandwich in one hand and a bunch of bananas in the other, sang "America" until the walls of the temple resounded with the patriotic air. The Bedouins smiled; they did more, they grinned—evidently for the first time in their lives—and the expression of their faces showed that they were wondering what manner of people we were. If not Christians, where did we come from? For they look upon all white-skinned people as their enemies, yet here were these Arabs laughing with us and even going so far as to forget they were there for "backsheesh."

In spite of our hurry to finish our meal that we might inspect the temples, for it was past midday, we found time to listen to Brother Williams' story of his humorous and exasperating experience that morning with a donkey man who persisted in pursuing him every step he took through the many zig-zag streets of Cairo—a most amusing and unique experience, which wound up with our dignified clerical friend suddenly turning upon his pursuer, glaring, howling and gesticulating to frighten him away. Not succeeding, he made a bold rush at him, and with arms extended, in broad Yorkshire English he consigned the poor donkey man to the dark regions which seemed to be a reality in his mind at that moment. This brought about the desired effect, for the poor terrified fellow hurriedly mounted his donkey and disappeared round the nearest corner.

The next thing that demanded our attention was the interior of the temple, its many walls and burial chambers. The temple itself is constructed of granite and alabaster and was no doubt in the remote ages used as a place of worship or assembly where the people made sacrifices in honor of their dead. The architcture was a marvel of simplicity and showed a perfection in the art of working the hardest kind of stone not attained at the present day.

We went through the long halls, passageways, and burial chambers; the interior of the latter was finished with alabaster, the transparency of which was very plainly seen by the light of the torch which our guide carried to show the way. In the floor of one of the halls is a deep well, said to have been connected at one time with the Nile. In it were found no less than nine statues of Chephren.

When we returned to the temple entrance after our inspection of its different features we were anxious to retrace our steps and observe more closely everything we had seen, but it was getting late and Cairo must be reached before sundown. We contented ourselves, however, as we planned to visit the great museum in Cairo before we left Egypt, where we would have the opportunity to see many of the relics connected with the temple.

Reluctantly we gathered up our belongings and prepared to depart. It was then that I longed to see somewhere nearby a real American camp where the weary Crusaders could live a tent life and build up for themselves in that calm restful atmosphere a new energy for the coming days.

At the call of Hassen, our dragoman, the Bedouins with their camels came up to the entrance of the temple, and amidst laughter and chatter at the clumsy way in which the Crusaders mounted their camels we commenced the slow ride over the desert to our great pyramid where we had left our carriage waiting.

It was here that we bade farewell to the place and the people. The Sheik was the first to push his way through the crowd that had gathered about the carriage. Assuming a look of sadness he reached out both hands to us "for a lastee America shakeeh and salaam." The Arab with whom I had conversed at the temple stood quite a distance away seemingly hesitating about coming up to where we were. Just as our carriage whipped up to start off he hurried towards me, took my hand and turned away. After I had reached the hotel I found he had dropped into the little bag which I wore attached to my belt an odd little charm. I shall aways keep it as a very precious souvenir of that one great day at the pyramids, and as a pleasant remembrance of my Arabian friend.

The other desert people kept shouting "Goobi-Ah-Ah-Backsheesh-Backsheesh," until the sound of their sharp ringing voices almost drove us frantic. As soon as we could recover our senses we good-naturedly gave them all the piastres we had. It seemed the most brotherly act we could do under the circumstances, for these protectors of the pyramids receive no recompense and depend entirely for their livelihood at certain seasons of the year (when the crops are not grown) upon the generosity of the tourist, which I have no doubt is often very meager.

One thing I observed, that the noise suddenly ceased and these people seemed satisfied with what we had done for them, which delighted us all, for they had placed us their debtors by a number of polite and very gracious favors.

As I turned back for one more look at all we were leaving behind, I could see that they had gone back to to the foot of the pyramid and were standing in a quiet and respectful attitude looking intently our way, watching us out of sight. A little to the left, separate from the rest, stood my Arabian friend with his face turned away toward the East.

Soon we were dreaming along the way—the border of the Nile—through the quiet and peace of the beautiful twilight, sensing the touch of sacredness in everything. Over the land like a benediction fell the pale golden rays of the setting sun—a misty veil of beauty, fields, river, trees, beasts and herdsmen. All seemed like phantoms of the dim past of thousands and thousands of years ago, far back of King Pharoah's time, and the Nile in its distinctive beauty added a new charm to the picturesqueness of that twilight dream.

"It flows through old, hushed Egypt and its sands
Like some grave, mighty thought threading a dream
And time and things, as in that vision, seem
Keeping along it their eternal stands.
Caves, pillars, pyramids, the shepherd bands
That roam through the young world the glory extreme
Of high Sesostris, and that southern beam
The laughing Queen that caught the world's great hand.
Then comes a mightier silence, stern and strong,
As of a world left empty of its throng,
And the void weighs on us; and then we wake
And run the fruitful stream lapsing along
Twixt villages, and think how we shall take
Our own calm journey on for human sake."

The Nile begins to rise at the end of May and continues to the middle of October. On the third week in August there is a festival held in its honor, probably a relic of the time when Rameses ordered sacrifices to be offered it on the 15th day of Thoth. This festival is announced to the people of Cairo by criers who go about through the city, crying the height of the Nile in the Nilometre at Rhoda. The Khedive, state officials, and crowds of people gather from many parts of Egypt to paticipate in this festival with song and music.

[Here followed fourteen verses of "Hymn to the Nile" written between the years 1300 B.C. and 1266 B.C. in the time of Moses by Ennana, a scribe of the temple.]

The king referred to in verse xii and xiv is Meneptah II, son of Rameses II, who is considered to have been the Pharaoh of The Exodus. It can be plainly seen in reading these verses how entirely unknown the sources of the Nile were at that time, and one can readily perceive how the mystery of its rising affected the Egyptians with the idea of an unseen hand that worked the miracle of giving the land a yearly blessing of water. Another interesting part of this hymn is the positive reference made to the pure and noble worship of one God, which shows that the author looked above the form of things into the Invisible.

Cairo was reached, and we were soon aroused from our dreams by the voices of the donkey boys who chased after our carriage shrieking, Ah! Ah! Coming! Coming! There were at least ten of them with their little donkeys gorgeously arrayed in bright saddle cloth and equipped with odd looking hump saddles. These little dusky-faced Arabs almost stopped our way in their wild efforts to induce us to take a ride to the museum which was nearby. They were soon lost sight of in a cloud of dust, and we drove on through the acacia-shadowed avenue past the mosques and a few stately dwellings into the very narrow streets where were small shops. In front, on the stoop, sat the vender selling the corn and fruits of Egypt. Handsome native women in loose garments clinging to their statuesque forms, carrying jars of water on their heads, moved along gracefully, timidly holding their veils over their faces, reminding one of the familiar pictures so widely associated with ancient Egypt. But to see them face to face in all their living charm of form and color transcended the most vivid fancy of my childhood. Some of the men were water carriers; they had strapped across their backs gourds for holding the water which they offered passersby as 'the gift of Allah'. Bright-eyed dusky-faced children with scanty garments and their heads decorated with gay-colored handkerchiefs played in the middle of the streets. All the way along at every turn there was something novel and picturesque to attract our attention. Tired and dusty as we were we would gladly have lingered at every point of interest, but duty called us back to the hotel where we were to hold a meeting that evening, and after an hour's rest, a bath, and a good dinner we found ourselves preparing for Crusade work.

It was out of the question to think of having a public meeting, but there was held in the drawing-room of the hotel one of a unique character which was most interesting to those who took part in it. At that time good seed was sown for future work of Brotherly Love in Egypt and most important connections were formed with the 'chosen few' who have the welfare of this ancient land at heart.

The next point of interest for us to visit was the great Museum of Cairo, the home of the mighty dead, to see the great Pharaoh, the hero and king of the past, whose body had rested for ages undiscovered amid the ruins of Thebes and after a lapse of 3000 years to again reappear on earth. The story of the royal find in the burial place of the kings at Thebes is a most interesting one. In 1881 forty mummies were found. The principal personages were the Queen of the Hyksos, time 2233 before Christ; four kings and three queens of the eighteenth dynasty, 1700 B.C. to 1433; three successive kings of the nineteenth dynasty, 1400 to 130, B.C., These were the great Pharaohs, Rameses II, his father Setti I, and his grandfather Rameses I.

The great difficulty was: how were the great dead to be removed to their final resting place, the Bulak Museum? Steamers had been sent for to come up to Luxor. The bodies and coffin-cases must be lifted up the shaft, carried down the difficult cliffside to the Theban plain, and ferried across the Nile, and then again borne on the shoulders of men to the Luxor riverside.

Three hundred Arabs were employed, and by earliest dawn they were busy in the removal and careful packing of the mummy-cases in matting and sail cloth. The work continued day and night. In forty-eight hours the coffins had been raised; and after six days' hard labor in the scorching sun all the cases were at the Nile bank. For three days and three nights brave Brugsch Bey, Kamal, Moutafian, and a few trustworthy Arabs watched over the boxes. What a thrilling sight it must have been as Brugsch Bey stood and watched the people carrying their royal burdens across the great Theban plain. His description of that picture is most interesting:

"I shall never forget the scene I witnessed, when standing at the mouth of the Der-el-Bahari shaft, I watched the strange train of helpers while they carried across that historical plain the bodies of the very kings who had constructed the very temples still standing, and of the priests who had officiated in them: the temple of Hatasou nearest; away across from it, Kurnah; further to the right the Ramesseum, where the great granite monolith lies face to the ground; further south, Medinet Habu; midway between, Der-el-Medinet; and then the twin colossi, the vocal Memnon, and his companion; then beyond all, more view of the plain; then the blue of the Nile and the Arabian hills far to the east; while slowly moving down the cliffs and across the plain, or in the boats crossing the Nile flood, were the sullen laborers carrying their ancient burdens.

"As the Red Sea opened and allowed Israel to pass; so opened the silence of the Theban plain, and allowed the royal funeral procession to pass, and then—all was hushed again. Go to Der-el-Bahari, and with a little imagination you will see it all spread out before you."

The mummies were packed aboard steamers and carried down the Nile. The news that Pharaoh was coming down the Nile had reached everywhere. Mr. Bugsch Bey writes "that one of the most striking things in the whole journey was the way in which there arose from all the land of Egypt an exceeding bitter cry, and women wailing and tearing their hair, men casting dust above their heads came crowding from the villages to the banks to make lamentation for Pharaoh."

Yes, the whole heart of Egypt and the old love for the mighty kings of the splendid days of old was deeply moved; and, as in the days more than 3000 years ago, with wailing and great weeping, the funeral barge had carried the dead kings up Nile to their sleep among the Theban hills, so today, with wailing and weeping and gnashing of teeth and all the signs of a national lamentation did the bodies of the mighty Pharoahs sail swiftly down through a land of mourning and sorrow and from their long repose in the Theban valley of the dead to their final rest at Cairo beside the shining Nile.

CHRONOLOGY

For fuller details readers are referred to Emmett A. Greenwalt: *California Utopia, Point Loma: 1897-1942.*

1847 July 6. Katherine Westcott Tingley born, Newbury Massachusetts. Father, Captain James P. Westcott, descendant of Stukeley Westcott, associated with Roger Williams, in the founding of Rhode Island: mother, née Susan Chase.

Early 1890's Do-Good Mission, East Side New York, for underprivileged and needy.

1894 Met William Q. Judge, then General Secretary of the American Section, The Theosophical Society. After Convention in Boston, April, 1895, he became President for life of The Theosophical Society in America.

1896 Succeeded W. Q. Judge as Outer Head of the Esoteric Section of The Theosophical Society in America. Organized and conducted world crusade of Theosophists from June 7, 1896, to April 4, 1897, beginning in Boston, Massachusetts, and culminating at Point Loma, California, where the cornerstone was laid of the "School for the Revival of the Lost Mysteries of Antiquity" on February 23, 1897, then on to New York. Countries visited were England, Ireland, Scotland, France, Holland, Germany, Austria, Switzerland, Italy, Greece, Egypt, India, Australia, New Zealand, Samoa, Canada, and back to the United States.

51 1898 January 13. Formation at New York City of The Universal Brotherhood Organization.

February 18. Convention of the T.S. in A. at Chicago, Illinois. The T.S. in A. merged with the Universal Brotherhood Organization to form The Universal Brotherhood and Theosophical Society, with Katherine Tingley as Leader and Official Head.

June. The Isis League of Art, Music and Drama established at New York.

August 23. Organized War Relief Corps in New York, and established emergency hospital at Montauk, Long Island, N.Y., for soldiers returning from Cuba. This work was officially commended by President William McKinley.

52 1899 February. Relief work in Cuba under the auspices of the International Brotherhood League, the practical humanitarian department of The Universal Brotherhood.

April 13. Congress of the Universal Brotherhood and Theosophcal Society opened at Point Loma, California. The Congress, which continued for ten days, was attended by delegates from many parts of the world.

August 29. Crusade to Europe with members of her Cabinet and others. Congress held at Stockholm, Sweden, September 13, attended by the King of Sweden and Norway. Germany, Denmark and England also visited.

October 6. Congress at the Royal Pavilion, Brighton, England.

October 10. Reception by members of the Universal Brotherhood at 19 Avenue Road, London (former home of H. P. Blavatsky), in honor of recovering possession of the property.

1900 February 13. Moved permanently to Point Loma, California, establishing International Headquarters of the Society there.

April 7. Building of Aryan Temple (later called Temple of Peace), dedicated to the memory of H. P. Blavatsky and William Q. Judge.

April 29. Laying of cornerstone of Isis Temple of Art, Music and Drama. Removal of all offices of the Society from 144 Madison Avenue, New York to Point Loma.

May 1. Dedication of International Lotus Home, and establishment of the Raja Yoga School.

1901 February 14. Daily lectures in Temple opened to public.

July 1. Building of the first open-air Greek Theater in the U.S.A. begun, completed in November. The Greek stoa was added in 1911.

August 3. Second visit to Cuba with staff for the purpose of selecting children for free education at the Point Loma school, returning on September 15 with 35 Cuban boys and girls chosen by Sr. don Emilio Bacardí, Mayor of the city of Santiago de Cuba.

1902 Purchase of Opera House in San Diego to be used for the work of the Isis Conservatory of Art, Music and Drama, and public dedication and renaming it Isis Theatre on May 18. Katherine Tingley gave regular Sunday Theosophical lectures there in ensuing years.

The Supreme Court of California affirmed verdict of the jury in awarding Katherine Tingley damages in her libel suit against the owner and publisher of the Los Angeles *Times*.

1903 Founding of the Raja-Yoga Academy (boarding school) and Raja Yoga free day school respectively near and in Santiago de Cuba.

1906 Raja Yoga School established in Pinar del Rio, Cuba.

1907 Visited with King Oscar of Sweden. Property on island of Visingsö purchased.

1909 January. Raja Yoga Academy opened in Santa Clara, Cuba.

1911 Prison reform work inaugurated and continued for many years. *The New Way*, monthly magazine at Point Loma for free distribution in prisons; edited by Herbert A. W. Coryn, M.R.C.S. until his death at Point Loma in 1927.

1913 Raja Yoga Summer-school established at Visingsö, Sweden.

International Theosophical Peace Congresses convened by Katherine Tingley at Visingsö, Sweden and at Point Loma. She and 25 of her students took part in the Twentieth World Peace Congress at The Hague, Holland.

1914 Toured with Governor Hunt of Arizona speaking against capital punishment.

1915 Parliament of Peace convened at Point Loma.

1919 Theosophical University organized and chartered under the laws of the State of California.

1920 March 22. Lectured at the Vista Alegre Theater in Santiago de Cuba.

1923-24-25-26-27-28 Lectured in U.S.A., England, Sweden, Holland and Germany.

1924 Theosophical Permanent Peace Congress held at Point Loma.

1929 July 11. Death of Katherine Tingley at Visingsö, Sweden, following an automobile accident at Osnabrück, Germany.